UNDERSTANDING ERITREA

MARTIN PLAUT

Understanding Eritrea

Inside Africa's Most Repressive State

OXFORD
UNIVERSITY PRESS

OXFORD
UNIVERSITY PRESS

Oxford University Press is a department of the
University of Oxford. It furthers the University's objective
of excellence in research, scholarship, and education
by publishing worldwide.

Oxford   New York

Auckland   Cape Town   Dar es Salaam   Hong Kong   Karachi
Kuala Lumpur   Madrid   Melbourne   Mexico City   Nairobi
New Delhi   Shanghai   Taipei   Toronto

With offices in

Argentina   Austria   Brazil   Chile   Czech Republic   France   Greece
Guatemala   Hungary   Italy   Japan   Poland   Portugal   Singapore
South Korea   Switzerland   Thailand   Turkey   Ukraine   Vietnam

Oxford is a registered trade mark of Oxford University Press
in the UK and certain other countries.

Published in the United States of America by
Oxford University Press
198 Madison Avenue, New York, NY 10016

Library of Congress Cataloging-in-Publication Data is available
Martin Plaut.
Understanding Eritrea: Inside Africa's Most Repressive State.
ISBN: 9780190669591

Printed in India on acid-free paper

*In memory of Dominique Jacquin-Berdal, whose early death deprived us all
of a great scholar and keen observer of the Horn of Africa*

CONTENTS

ABBREVIATIONS

Derg	The movement that seized power in Ethiopia in 1974. The term means 'committee' and was shorthand for the Coordinating Committee of the Armed Forces, Police, and Territorial Army
ELF	Eritrean Liberation Front
EPLF	Eritrean People's Liberation Front
EU	European Union
TPLF	Tigray People's Liberation Front
OLF	Oromo Liberation Front
PFDJ	People's Front for Democracy and Justice (the name of the EPLF after 1994)
UN	United Nations
UNHCR	United Nations High Commission for Refugees
UNMEE	United Nations Mission to Ethiopia and Eritrea

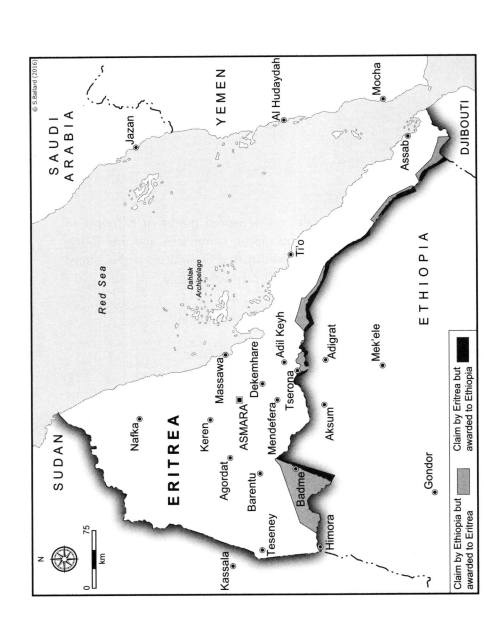

1

INTRODUCTION

The capital of Eritrea, Asmara, situated on a high plateau, is one of the most pleasant cities in Africa. Its quiet streets, its cool, welcoming bars and its friendly people make it a joy to visit. The Italians who colonised it left an indelible mark on the vibrant culture. Delicious traditional food is served alongside Italian cuisine. The streets are lined with some of the best-preserved Modernist architecture: a legacy of the Fascist era and Italy's determination to make Eritrea a fine gateway to an empire that included Ethiopia. A railway links the city with the port of Massawa, bending and twisting down a steep escarpment—descending more than two kilometres to the plain below. The beaches and islands that dot the coast are pristine and could easily compete with the Sinai for the tourist trade.

Life for ordinary Eritreans is tough. Farmers plough the unforgiving soil, hoping that last year's rains will be repeated. Most of the population work in subsistence agriculture, but there is also time for celebration. Over the weekend the roads surrounding Asmara are alive with cyclists. The country's team is one of the best on the continent and cycling is a passion. The lanes of the villages and cities echo to the sound of music. Barren, rugged mountain ranges fade into the distance. Flashes of brilliant reds and iridescent blues and greens mark the flight of birds through the green-grey bush. There is great diversity among the country's ethnic groups. Yet given the country's undoubted natural beauty and rich cultural heritage, why do as many as 5,000 Eritreans flee across its borders every month? What explains their determination to leave at almost any price—risking the dangers of crossing the Sahara and the Mediterranean to escape the land they love? Eritrea is not at war. Unlike Syria or Yemen it is not racked by civil conflict. Its cities and countryside are peaceful. The country is poor, but then so are many other African states, yet they are not haemorrhaging people.

The answer lies in politics. This nation of 3.5–6.5 million people (no one knows for certain: the only complete census was taken in 1931) is held in servitude. There is just one legal political party and even this holds no regular congresses: the last took place in 1994. The president, Isaias Afwerki, is an autocrat who brooks no opposition. Opinions that diverge from the official line are simply not tolerated. The last independent journalists and editors were rounded up in 2001, their papers closed. The Constitution, written and approved by the Constituent Assembly (or parliament) has never been brought into force.

A United Nations Commission of Inquiry on Eritrea concluded in 2015 that the Eritrean government engages in 'systemic, widespread and gross human rights violations' carried out in a 'context of a total lack of rule of law.' Fear hangs over the Eritrean people; both inside the country and among the diaspora. This is the product of the ruthless repression that the regime has meted out. There is, as the Norwegian academic, Kjetil Tronvoll, put it, an Eritrean 'Gulag archipelago': political prisons, detention centres and labour camps which stretch across the country like a chain of islands. Some are formal prisons, others converted stores and some even makeshift facilities, often shipping containers. Here prisoners languish for years at a time. Brutal treatment is routinely administered and there is no recourse to any form of legal action. None of these detainees ever sees a court, let alone a defence lawyer.

Yet even this would not have driven people across the border and into the loneliness and despair of exile. To understand why they flee in such numbers one has to grasp just what it is young people face. They are conscripted into the military with no guarantee that it will ever end. National Service, as it is called, is indefinite. Some have served for decades, yet have no prospect of release. Pay is derisory, conditions are grindingly tough and there is routine abuse from officers. Women are in danger of sexual abuse and frequently used as servants.

This phenomenon is rooted in Eritrea's extraordinary history. Its people fought for their freedom from Ethiopia for thirty years, achieving independence in 1991 and international recognition as a sovereign state two years later. For much of this period the nation has been led by Isaias Afwerki, known universally as Isaias (Eritreans and Ethiopians are known by their first names, and frequently by a nickname given to them early in their lives). His forceful personality and intolerance of opposition were arguably critical to winning the war against Ethiopia, but when independence came, it was another story.

At first relations between a post-independent Eritrea and the new Ethiopian government were good. Gradually, however, they soured, then erupted into full-scale warfare. In 1998–2000 these neighbours, who shared so much in common, fought one of the bloodiest conflicts in Africa since the Second World War. Although ostensibly over a minor border village, there were far deeper roots to the war. These go back to the history of the region and the history of political parties that still dominate both countries. For this reason I have spent what readers might consider an inordinate time explaining the complex relationship between guerrilla movements that were rarely mentioned in the wider world before they seized power in both countries in 1991.

I have attempted to lay out how this came about. Much is still veiled and obscure. This is hardly surprising when Eritrea refuses to allow foreign news organisation to have correspondents based in the country. Nor are the UN agencies given much greater freedom: their operations inside Eritrea are severely curtailed. Few sources of accurate, open information are therefore available. And Eritreans (as well as Ethiopians) are culturally disposed to being closed and secretive. Winston Churchill once said of the Soviet Union that it was a riddle wrapped in a mystery inside an enigma. I hope in this book to clarify some of Eritrea's riddles.

2

A DIFFICULT HISTORY

Down the centuries fleets have sailed past Eritrea's shores; navies have used her harbours and armies have trampled her soil. Greeks, Saudis, Yemenis and Egyptians all left their mark before the Ottoman Turks extended their rule to the Eritrean coast in the sixteenth century. Its ports were important links in trade with countries as far afield as India. But Eritrea's recent destiny has been shaped, above all, by its proximity to Ethiopia.

An exposure to these foreign influences forged an Eritrean social entity and a distinct Eritrean consciousness. This identity has always been complex precisely because it reflects a diverse population. Eritrea's peoples are divided roughly equally between two major religions: Islam and Christianity. They speak nine different languages. Most of the eastern and western lowland areas are inhabited by predominantly Muslim ethnic groups. The majority of highlanders belong to the Tigrinya ethnic group and are Orthodox Christians.

The coastal lowlands are inhabited by the Afar in the east, closely linked to Afar in Djibouti and Ethiopia. Further west-wards, along the Danakil desert, are the Saho, whose neighbours are the Tigrinya population. They inhabit the centre of the country, from the port of Massawa onto the plateau and to the Ethiopian border. The Tigrinya people make up about half of all Eritreans and live in towns such as Asmara, Mendefera and Adi Qeyih. The Rashaida, also on the coastal plain, have family ties across the Sudanese border. Inhabiting a large part of the western plains are the Tigre, who are the second largest ethnic group. They live in the towns of Nakfa, Agordat and Tessenai. Between the Tigre and the Tigrinya are the Bilen, who cluster around the town of Keren—the strategically important gateway from Sudan into the highlands. Three other smaller ethnic groups live on Eritrea's borders with Sudan and Ethiopia. They are the Hedareb, Nara and Kunama.

While most of the lowland peoples are Muslim the highlanders tend to be Christian. The Kunama have their own ancient religion and suffered long years of persecution from both Christians and Muslims as a result. The Eritrean government recognises these nine ethnic groups, each of which speaks their own language. But Eritrea does have other ethnicities, including the Jeberti–Tigrinya-speaking Muslims who are not officially recognised. There is also a remnant of the Italian colonial community and once there was a small number of Jews, most of whom came from Yemen, but hardly any remain. Since 2001 hundreds of thousands of Eritreans have fled their country and this makes it difficult to provide an accurate estimate of the ethnic balance.

The Christian agriculturalists of the central highlands share a common language, religion and ethnic background with the Ethiopian region of Tigray, just across the border. Intermarriage between Tigrinya speakers of Eritrea and Tigray has traditionally been common. These areas had been part of the Ethiopian Empire intermittently for most of the first millennium AD. The mainly Muslim lowland pastoralists, on the other hand, had little in common with them. Rather, they looked to Sudan or across the Red Sea to Saudi Arabia or Yemen.

A DIFFICULT HISTORY

The complex identities of the ethnic groups who made Eritrea their home were gradually united as a single nation. Colonisation by Italy and Ethiopia played critical roles in this process. So too did Britain, which captured the territory from Italy during the Second World War. This was no simple process—rather it was an evolution that took place over the centuries; in many ways it is still continuing. Recent Eritrean history comprises five periods: Italian colonialism (1886–1941), followed by British military rule (1942–1952), Federation with Ethiopia (1952–1960), the struggle for liberation (1961–1991) and the post-Independence era (1991–present).

Eritrea's roots

The kingdoms of Ethiopia had a major influence over their northern neighbour. When they were powerful, Ethiopian rulers extended their influence over parts of Eritrea; when they were weak their control ebbed and the rulers returned to their heartlands in Aksum and Tigray. By the end of the nineteenth century Ethiopia was barely more than a loose confederation of kingdoms. The Ethiopian empire was alternatively dominated by Amhara or Oromo princes from the provinces of Gondar and Wollo in the centre of the country, or by Tigrean rulers from the northern region of Tigray, which at times included the Tigrinya-speaking areas of what is now Eritrea. The empire's boundaries were fluid. When Tigrayan princes were in the ascendancy they extended their influence towards Eritrea's Red Sea Coast, exacting tribute from the Muslim lowland chiefs around Massawa or in the West.

After 1557 the coastal plain of Eritrea became part of the expanding Ottoman Empire. For most of the seventeenth and eighteenth centuries the rulers of the coast were appointed by the Ottoman Pasha of Jeddah, sporadically acknowledging the overlordship of Tigray's rulers. As the Ottoman Empire declined,

Egypt inherited its place along the Red Sea coast. Britain had used the Eritrean coast as a means of attacking Ethiopia in 1868 after the emperor Tewodros II took captive the British consul, Charles Duncan Cameron. With his fleet anchored in the Gulf of Zula, just south of the port of Massawa, Lt. Gen. Sir Robert Napier led a vast army into the Ethiopian interior to free Cameron and a group of hostages jailed with him. Napier finally took the fortress of Magdala, and the emperor committed suicide. The captives were freed and the British left, taking with them quantities of historical and religious artefacts.

Egypt had taken Massawa in the 1800s and then attempted to extend its influence into the interior. In the 1870s, the Tigrean emperor Yohannis IV (1872–1889) defeated two Egyptian invasions of the Eritrean highlands. Subsequently he believed that in return for allowing the evacuation of Egyptian garrisons from Sudan after the rise of the Mahdi, he had British and Egyptian agreement to take over Massawa.

In the event, Britain (worried about expanding French influence in Africa) instead encouraged Italy to take Massawa in 1885. The Italians were ideal candidates to play this role: they already had a small Eritrean foothold. Rome had established an agricultural concession in the western Eritrean town of Keren in 1867, and then purchased the port of Assab from local rulers in 1869. This was not done without difficulty. It was a period of Ethiopian strength, with the Tigray region in the ascendency and trading through the port of Massawa, which it indirectly controlled.

As the British former colonial civil servant Gerald Kennedy Trevaskis puts it, 'Italy created Eritrea by an act of surgery: by severing its different peoples from those with whom their past had been linked and by grafting the amputated remnants to each other under the title of Eritrean.' The Italians ruled Eritrea from 1886 until their imperial moment was extinguished by Britain during the Second World War.

A DIFFICULT HISTORY

Yohannis felt betrayed, the more so as Italy promptly attempted to use the port as a base from which to extend its influence into Ethiopia. These hopes were dashed when the Italians were crushed in 1896 by the Ethiopian forces of Emperor Menelik at the battle of Adua. The defeat was a major blow to the Italians, who lost thousands of troops, both killed and captured. Italy was humiliated since the defeat represented one of the few victories 'native' troops inflicted on a European power during the colonial era. Rome had little option but to accept this reverse, and signed treaties with the emperor in 1900, 1902 and 1908 establishing the border between its new colony, Eritrea, and Ethiopia.

With the rise of fascism under Mussolini, Italy was determined to avenge its loss of face and extend its presence in the Horn of Africa. In October 1935 Italy invaded Ethiopia from the territory it controlled in Eritrea. Thousands of Eritrean local troops—'askaris'—fought alongside their Italian colonial masters. Despite the League of Nation's condemnation of the Italians it was not until the outbreak of the Second World War that external powers took a decisive stand against their aggression. Using tanks, aerial bombardment and nerve gas the Italians captured Addis Ababa on 5 May 1936. The emperor left for exile in Britain but Ethiopian guerrilla forces continued the fight. In February 1941 British troops, supported by a large contingent of Indian soldiers and including Free French and Ethiopian forces, attacked Eritrea from Sudan. For over two months there was a fierce battle around the town of Keren, which was heavily defended. Italian troops were dug in along the rocky mountainsides guarding the pass into the town. In March the Allied soldiers captured the town—an event that was hailed in the British press as a major victory over the Axis forces. They drove on to Asmara, which fell on 1 April 1941.

On 5 May Haile Selassie returned to Addis Ababa exactly five years to the day from when it had been occupied by Italy. He was returned to his throne by a combined force of British, South African, Indian and Sudanese troops fighting alongside Ethiopian patriots.

While Ethiopia was independent once more, the international community was left with the problem of what to do with Eritrea, which was under temporary British Military Administration. Italian colonialism had brought with it some of the benefits of European rule, in the shape of modern port facilities, roads and railways. The city of Asmara had developed into a pleasant town, with broad streets, an opera house and fine government buildings. By the time the Italians were driven out by the Allied forces in 1941, they left behind a far more developed state than the feudal empire that had previously existed in Ethiopia.

The British disbanded the large Eritrean colonial army and the Italian fascist militia, but most Italian civil servants remained in place. Saddled with huge post-war debts the British sold off parts of Eritrea's infrastructure. At the same time the United States was allowed to establish a strategically important satellite listening post at Kagnew, close to the airport of the capital, Asmara. From this base up to 3,000 American personnel did vital work during the Cold War. They tracked Soviet rocket launches; a practice that continued until 1977.

The British struggled to come up with an effective administration for Eritrea. Sometimes London favoured partition of the country into Muslim and Christian blocs and at other times looked to establish British control of areas of Ethiopia. This exacerbated tensions between these two communities, each of which represented approximately half of the population. Eritrean politics divided along religious lines, the Muslim League seeking independence and the mainly Christian Unionist Party favouring links with Ethiopia. In 1946 there were inter-communal riots, which elders from both communities worked hard to bring under control. In 1947 political parties were legalised.

A DIFFICULT HISTORY

Two years later London presented the United Nations with a plan that envisaged the division of Eritrea, with the western lowlands going to Sudan and the remainder to Ethiopia. The United Nations refused to endorse the scheme. Britain, fed up with attempting to resolve the future of Eritrea, turned the issue over to the UN which sent a Commission to visit Eritrea, seeking the views of its people. In 1952 the UN finally decided that the territory should be federated with Ethiopia, while continuing to exercise considerable autonomy over its own affairs. There matters might have rested. However, the emperor's absolutist rule alienated the Eritrean population by imposing on it a series of decrees and unilateral actions. These included outlawing the teaching of Eritrean languages, replacing them with Amharic (the official language of the empire) and dismantling industries and removing them to Addis Ababa. Eritrean trade unions and political parties (allowed under the British military administration) were crushed; neither was acceptable in the emperor's Ethiopia.

Armed resistance to Ethiopian rule erupted on 1 September 1961, when a bandit turned rebel, Hamid Idris Awate, and eleven of his supporters were involved in a clash with a police unit. Opponents of Addis Ababa formed the Eritrean Liberation Front (ELF), which moved from isolated resistance to open warfare. From then on the conflict with Ethiopia escalated until it became the largest rebellion on the African continent, involving tens of thousands of combatants. At the same time there was, at first, still considerable support inside Eritrea for unity with Ethiopia, particularly from among the Christian highlanders. In November 1962, after intense pressure from Addis Ababa, the Federation was dissolved, and Eritrea was absorbed into Ethiopia. This served to spur on the opposition, led at first by the ELF, whose support came mainly from the Muslim community, although some Christian highlanders, including the future leader of Eritrea, Isaias Afwerki, were also drawn into membership.

The first decade of the armed struggle from 1961 to 1974 was largely confined to the Muslim lowlands. Disputes within the ELF and hostility towards Christian recruits resulted in the formation of the Eritrean People's Liberation Front (EPLF) in the early 1970s. The EPLF rejected ethnic differences and stood for a secular and socialist state, but the majority of its support came from the Christian highlands. The lowlanders' backing for the ELF was predominantly motivated by a sense of alienation from a highland government, which spoke a different language and practised a different religion. An uneasy truce between the two movements culminated in a bitter civil war that the EPLF finally won in 1981, driving the ELF out of Eritrea. From then on the ELF was forced to base itself in and operate as best it could from neighbouring Sudan.

Despite these divisions, Ethiopia's campaign against the Eritrean rebels fared badly. Discontent inside the Ethiopian army over the conduct of the war and the handling of a devastating famine led to the overthrow of the emperor in 1974. Haile Selassie was replaced by a military committee, known as the Derg. In time this came under the dictatorial rule of Mengistu Haile Mariam. The emperor was finally murdered, with his body buried beneath a latrine in the grounds of the imperial palace.

At first it appeared as if the Derg was willing to see a settlement of the Eritrean question. But after initial discussions with the Eritreans failed, the war was continued and intensified. The events of 1974 led to a second, equally important development. Students from the northern Ethiopian province of Tigray, angered by the lack of development of their area, decided to launch their own campaign against the rulers in Addis Ababa. Building on the ancient claims of Tigray as the centre of the Ethiopian state, they fought to break rule from the capital. In 1975 the Tigray People's Liberation Front (TPLF) was formed and launched its own war against the Ethiopian authorities.

Initially relations between the EPLF and TPLF were cordial, with the Eritreans providing support to the Tigrayan rebels, but this relationship soon deteriorated.

Nationalism in Eritrea and northern Ethiopia

On the face of it the EPLF and the TPLF had much in common. They both opposed Ethiopian absolutism, whether exercised by Haile Selassie or Mengistu Haile Mariam. Both organisations were Marxist in outlook. In reality, however, the forms of national identity that the two movements pursued, and in a sense embodied, were rather different. These factors contributed to hostility and distrust that have afflicted their relations ever since. The Eritreans saw their struggle as an anti-colonial movement designed to regain a lost political independence. The TPLF leadership, on the other hand, moved from a Tigrayan nationalism to an acceptance that they were part of the Ethiopian state. The TPLF came to see their rightful place as being at the heart of events in Ethiopia. They regarded the current regime as an oppressive state, which should be overthrown.

The EPLF attempted to mobilise Eritrean opinion irrespective of religion, but came up against considerable difficulties. Not all of the Christians in the highlands supported the cause of independence, and as late as 1982 some were still willing to act as an armed militia for the Ethiopian administration. Outside the highlands, despite the terror employed by the Mengistu regime, a majority within the Kunama and the Afar people were at best ambivalent about the EPLF. Some actually supported continued unity with Ethiopia and thousands of Kunama served in the Ethiopian army. As a result the EPLF had to fight a vigorous campaign within its own community to win their support, or at least acquiescence.

While it recognised and even celebrated Eritrea's ethnic diversity, the EPLF resolutely refused to allow ethnicity to undermine its campaign for an independent state. This is not to suggest that ethnicity played no part in the Front's activities; great care was taken to represent the whole of the population within the leadership, even when they were not as well represented among its membership. At the same time critics of the movement question just how much real influence key Muslim members of the EPLF exercised. The EPLF certainly spent a good deal of time and effort inculcating a wider sense of Eritrean identity in its new recruits.

For the TPLF mobilisation in Tigray was relatively simple, since it could call upon an existing concept of Tigrayan nationalism in all the areas in which it operated. They shared a common language and mode of livelihood. Apart from a few highland Muslims all Tigrayans were Orthodox Christians. The TPLF's activities were an attempt to end Amhara rule. In Tigrayan eyes the Amhara had usurped the traditional power base of Ethiopian society, and transferred it from the ancient Tigrayan capital of Axum to Addis Ababa. Haile Selassie's rule was widely (and correctly) perceived as essentially Amhara. In its first political programme, released in 1976, the TPLF specified that it was fighting for the independence of Tigray from Ethiopia. Shortly thereafter a TPLF congress repudiated the manifesto, but did not make this public. This has been a recurrent issue for the movement, and has also been seized upon by its critics.

Since the TPLF's war aims, at least in the beginning, centred on achieving power in Tigray itself, its successes against the forces of the Derg posed something of a problem for the movement, and led to considerable internal debate. Would it be satisfied with capturing Tigray, or would a hostile government in Addis Ababa require the movement to fight to control all of Ethiopia? By early 1989 the TPLF exercised almost total control over the Tigrayan countryside and was enjoying increasing success against Ethiopian troops in garrisons across the province. In February 1989 TPLF forces, bolstered by an EPLF armoured brigade, took the area around Endaselasie, in western Tigray. Within two weeks garrisoned towns across the province were abandoned, sometimes without a fight.

The TPLF had achieved its initial objectives and held most of Tigray. The question now was whether to press on to Addis Ababa. The movement had by this time established the Ethiopian People's Revolutionary Democratic Front (EPRDF), together with a number of other Ethiopian organisations, with the aim of taking power in Addis Ababa. Its leadership had ambitions to rule the whole of Ethiopia but were frustrated by many of its own supporters who (to use Lenin's famous phrase) voted with their feet. In 1990 some 10,000 TPLF fighters spontaneously walked home. After months of protracted discussion the leadership managed to convince its followers that they should continue prosecuting the war. Tigrayan nationalism was, at least for the time being, to be subordinated within a wider Ethiopian identity.

The EPLF and the TPLF therefore relied upon completely different nationalisms. The Eritrean struggle for independence had generated a powerful sense of collective identity, as did the increasingly genocidal responses of the Derg towards Eritreans during the 1980s. It was nationalism forged in blood and with a clear objective in mind: the freedom of Eritrea. Moreover, it was a nationalism that could justly claims that it was shaped by its own experience of colonialism. The Tigrayans also had much to be proud of. They could hark back to past greatness, including the rule of the last 'Tigrayan' emperor and to a history of rebellions against imperial rule. The most important of these was a peasant uprising of 1943 against Haile Selassie's autocratic rule. Known as the 'woyane' rebellion (a term meaning 'revolt') it was the event from which the TPLF took its inspiration. But while Eritrean nationalism was clearly associated with a nation state, Tigrayan nationalism played a difficult balancing act—recognising the aspirations of the Tigrayan people, but within the framework of the wider Ethiopian state. It was a problem that was to dog the relationship between the TPLF and the EPLF.

Co-operation and confrontation

Opposition to the dictatorial rule exercised from Addis Ababa temporarily united the two liberation movements, but divisions existed on a number of grounds, including ideology, strategy and tactics. Over time these grew in importance.

In 1974, as the founders of the TPLF were preparing to launch an armed struggle, they had contacted the Eritrean movements, an obvious source of assistance. They sought support from the EPLF, rather than the ELF. This was partly because another group of Tigrayans (The Tigray Liberation Front) had been established in 1972–73 and had formed a prior alliance with the ELF. From the EPLF the TPLF obtained military training as well as arms, and, significantly, two EPLF veterans. They were Mahari Haile (who took the field name 'Mussie' and went on to be the first military commander) and Yemane Kidane (known as 'Jamaica') who became a member of the Ethiopian government. The first group of TPLF trainees, twenty in all, was deployed to Eritrea at the same time.

This co-operation was fruitful and the Tigrayans learned a good deal from the Eritreans. However, not all of it was to their liking. Ideology came to play a significant part in their differences. On the face of it both movements shared a radical perspective; in reality this was more of an impediment than a spur to unity. The EPLF's Marxism tended to be mostly third-worldist: long on anti-imperialist rhetoric and slogans. It considered the Soviet bloc 'strategic allies', even though they never received direct assistance from Moscow. States in the region that were close to the Soviets, like South Yemen, provided some training and support. This ceased after the Derg seized power in Ethiopia in 1974, since it won the backing of the Soviet Union.

A DIFFICULT HISTORY

The TPLF, on the other hand, was influenced by Maoism, and admired Albania as an example of an anti-Soviet socialist state. In the early 1980s Meles Zenawi rose to authority in the movement, and in 1984 the Marxist-Leninist League of Tigray (MLLT) was formed, as a vanguard party within the TPLF. This vanguard party established links with what it saw as 'genuine' Eritrean groups, notably a former faction of the ELF called the Democratic Movement for the Liberation of Eritrea. The Democratic Movement was allowed to continue to have bases in the Tigray region until about 1996, much to the annoyance of the EPLF.

The United States had openly backed the emperor, Haile Selassie, but his fall in 1974 and the assumption of power by the Derg led to a recalibration in international relations. At first Moscow only reluctantly supported the new regime, since it was a military dictatorship. But in the end the Soviet Union decided to back the Ethiopians. This tested the EPLF's ideological commitment. However, the EPLF resisted labelling the Soviet Union as imperialist, realising that they might one day need its support as a permanent member of the Security Council if they were to gain international recognition as an independent state. The Tigrayans had no such inhibition, since Ethiopia was already a fully-fledged member of the UN. The TPLF therefore condemned the Soviets as imperialist. Arcane as such arguments might now seem, they were an important source of friction between the two movements.

Ideology was not the only question to divide them; they also fell out over military tactics. While the TPLF's military strategy was one of mobile guerrilla warfare, the EPLF combined mobility with fixed positional warfare, based on a securely defended rear area. In this base area they established a considerable infrastructure, including schools, hospitals and workshops. As the Eritreans moved towards more conventional forms of warfare, the Tigrayans became increasingly critical of their tactics.

Matters came to a head during Ethiopia's 'Red Star' campaign of 1982 against the Eritreans. It was the most sustained offensive the government forces ever undertook and came within an ace of capturing the EPLF's base area, and with it Nakfa, the last town in rebel hands. Tigrayan fighters training with the EPLF were called on to go into action. This was apparently done without the permission of the TPLF Central Committee, who were furious at not being asked. After heroic efforts their combined forces just managed to repel the Ethiopian onslaught. Casualties were heavy, however, and the TPLF was deeply critical of the EPLF, accusing the Eritreans of being willing to sacrifice its fighters to secure Nakfa.

According to senior members of the TPLF, the Eritreans wanted TPLF fighters to remain in Eritrea to defend their positions. By this time, however, the TPLF leadership were determined to overthrow the Derg. Their strategy, therefore, was to forge alliances with other Ethiopian opposition movements and to take the military struggle south to the gates of the capital. The TPLF therefore withdrew their fighters from Eritrea, a decision that was resented by their allies. Worse was to follow.

In the mid-1980s the simmering differences culminated in a major public row. Insults were exchanged. The TPLF defined the EPLF as 'social imperialist'; the EPLF in turn labelled the TPLF as 'childish'. The row masked a serious theoretical difference with major political ramifications for the national question in Ethiopia. The issue was which of its peoples had the right to self-determination up to, and including, secession. It had been a critical issue for the student radicals at Addis Ababa University in the 1960s and 1970s—many of whom went on to lead the Eritrean and Tigrayan liberation movements. The TPLF recognised Eritrea's unique status as a former colonial state. At the same time they promoted the right to secession of the various nationalities within Ethiopia and—far more controversially—of those within Eritrea as well. During its exchange of polemics

with the EPLF from 1985, the TPLF stated that 'a truly democratic' Eritrea would have to respect 'the right of its own nationalities up to and including secession'.

This appalled and infuriated the EPLF, which argued that it
was precisely because Eritrea was a former colonial state that they
had the right to independence. They declared that Ethiopian
nationalities had a right to self-determination, but *not* to independence, as this was conditional on a colonial experience. The
EPLF was aware that any widening of the definition of self-
determination to include independence for Ethiopian nationalities would detract from Eritrea's special status, as a colonially
defined territory. Moreover, giving Eritrean nationalities the
right to secede would jeopardise Eritrea's future cohesion, not
least because the Tigrayan and Afar peoples live on both sides of
the border.

The TPLF said that the EPLF's refusal to recognise the right
of its own nationalities was an example of its 'undemocratic'
nature. For this reason the TPLF regarded its relationship with
the EPLF as tactical, rather than enduring, and consequently the
TPLF provided support to other Eritrean movements, such as
the Democratic Marxist League of Eritrea.

According to EPLF documents, the TPLF's flirtation with
other movements came as a surprise and a disappointment. It led
to a rupture in their alliance:

> ...the TPLF had concluded that the EPLF was not a democratic organ-
> isation and that its relationship with the EPLF was 'tactical'. The
> EPLF had thought that its co-operation with the TPLF was genuine
> and not based on temporary tactical considerations. And so, when the
> TPLF's secret stand became public the EPLF realised its naiveté and
> although it did not regret its past actions, decided to break its relation-
> ship with the TPLF and not enter into polemics with it.

It was at this critical juncture, when relations were at their
most difficult, that the movements sought to resolve the ques-

tion of just where the border ran between Eritrea and Tigray. For a long time this had appeared of little real importance since both rebel groups ranged freely across the border, as did the Ethiopian army. Very little has been heard of the negotiations that took place in late 1984, but a founder member of the TPLF, Ghidey Zeratsion, offered an insight into the negotiations. He indicates why the issue became so critical for the Eritreans:

> The border issue was raised for the first time at the meeting between the TPLF and EPLF in November 1984. At this meeting, the EPLF raised the issue and wanted to demarcate the boundary based on international agreements and documents. The areas under consideration were Badme, Tsorena-Zalambessa, and Bada. The TPLF agreed that there are areas between Ethiopia and Eritrea where they are not clearly demarcated. At the same time it argued that it was not prepared for such discussion and had not made documentary studies on the issue. Furthermore, the TPLF argued that it was not in a position to sign border agreements on behalf of Ethiopia because it did not have the legitimacy to do so. And hence, the TPLF proposed to maintain the existing administrative areas as they are and prepare the necessary documents for the final demarcation after the fall of the Derg. The EPLF was convinced by the argument and both agreed to postpone the demarcation and maintain the existing administrative regions.

> One may ask why the border issue was so important for EPLF while it was still trenched in the Sahel area?

> The EPLF was very much constrained by its ability to get recruits for its army. It has been rounding up and forcefully recruiting people all over Eritrea. In such a situation, border areas like Badme were safe havens for people who wanted to escape recruitment. At the same time, there are a number of Eritreans living in these areas who were attractive for EPLF's quest of recruits. As a result, the EPLF was intruding these border areas and provoking a reaction from the TPLF. At one instant the two fronts were at the verge of war if the EPLF had not withdrawn. The EPLF could not afford to open another front while it was confined in the Sahel trenches by the Derg's army.

By early 1985 relations between the two movements had become mired in distrust.

As the relationship deteriorated the TPLF began providing assistance to Eritrean movements hostile to the EPLF.

In June 1985 the EPLF decided to teach the TPLF a brutal lesson. The Eritreans cut the TPLF's supply lines to the Sudan that passed through their territory. This was done at the height of one of the worst famines in modern times, denying Tigrayans access to food aid at a crucial juncture. Little was said publicly about the incident at the time, but it is not hard to imagine the animosity that it generated. The TPLF responded with characteristic efficiency, mobilising 100,000 peasants to build an alternative route through to Sudan that did not go via Eritrea. The cost was high: many perished in the construction.

While the EPLF leadership has been silent about these events, Tigrayans recall it with great bitterness. As one put it: 'the EPLF behaviour was a savage act... I do not hesitate to categorise it as a "savage act". It must be recorded in history like that!' This anger is hardly surprising: the closure of the border caused thousands of Tigrayans to die of starvation before the alternative road could be completed.

Despite this rupture the imperatives of war against the Derg forced the movements to co-operate with each other. By 1987 both Fronts had had considerable military success, but further advances required co-ordinated action. In April 1988, after four days of discussions in Khartoum, a joint statement was issued, indicating that their differences had been set aside. At the same time there was no suggestion that they had been resolved. This was a military pact, not an alliance of like-minded organisations—a point stressed by the TPLF's Yemane Kidane. The two fronts were not reconciled ideologically or politically: 'Never, never. Only a military relationship. Ideologically never, politically never. We maintained our differences. So we always say it is a tactical relationship, not a strategic relationship. If they call it strategic, it is up to them.' Military co-operation led to military success. In May 1991 the Eritreans finally took their capital, Asmara, after a war lasting thirty years. They also accompanied the Ethiopian rebels as they marched into Addis Ababa, providing troops and artillery. With both capitals in rebel hand, bonds between the EPLF and TPLF appeared strong. Isaias Afwerki became president of Eritrea, while his opposite number, the TPLF leader, Meles Zenawi, took control of Ethiopia. Their members had fought side by side against appalling odds. The leadership of the movements had come to know and rely upon one another. Past differences had been smoothed over, even if they had not been forgotten. Divisions remained, but there appeared a chance that these could be overcome, given the goodwill that existed.

Agreements were made in 1991 and 1993 allowing the free movement of labour across their common border; for Eritrea's use of Ethiopian currency, the Birr; for regulated Ethiopian trade through the port of Assab to minimise the effects of Ethiopia's loss of its coastline, and so on. Above all, the TPLF honoured its promise to support an Eritrean independence referendum in 1993, despite hostility from many sections of Ethiopian society. When Meles Zenawi went to Asmara to take part in the formal declaration of independence in late May 1993 in his capacity as an Ethiopian head of state, he offered a warning to his audience. The speech appealed for reconciliation, but Meles went on to call for both sides not to 'scratch the wounds' of the past. It was a timely warning. Despite this discordant note his words were well received in Asmara and relations between the two capitals appeared to be on a firm footing.

Indeed, co-operation between the two governing parties was so strong that a senior Eritrean seriously looked forward to the day when the two countries were united once more in a regional organisation. Amare Tekle, the former Referendum Commissioner of Eritrea, optimistically recommended the establishment of a 'cooperative relationship between Eritrea and Ethiopia as a necessary first step for the creation of a Horn of Africa Community.' Diplomats of the two countries occasionally even represented each other's interests in international fora. Relations—at least on the surface—appeared warm. Extraordinary as such sentiments might seem today, they genuinely reflected the optimism of the time.

* * *

What had begun as a supportive relationship between two liberation movements was to sour badly. Ideological differences had festered and finally turned to open hostility. It had taken the exigencies of war to get the EPLF and TPLF to work together once more. The result had been an extraordinary success: the rulers in Addis Ababa had been overthrown and new regimes had emerged. There was, for once, a real chance to move forward and establish a positive relationship between the two nations. It was a rare moment of optimism in the Horn of Africa, but it was not to last.

3

THE THORNY RELATIONSHIP WITH ETHIOPIA

Growing tensions

Relations between Eritrea and Ethiopia are critical for the communities living on both sides of their mutual border. Their long and tangled history makes this inevitable. The culture and economies of communities on this 1,000 km frontier are naturally intertwined. They lived, traded and married each other for centuries before any boundary was drawn on a map. So it will perhaps come as some surprise that even at the moment of victory over the Derg the first cracks appeared in the relationship between the two movements that represented them.

On taking Asmara the EPLF expelled the Ethiopian army of occupation from its soil. It also insisted that tens of thousands of Ethiopian citizens who had been involved in the Ethiopian administration leave as well. Between 1991 and 1992 around 120,000 Ethiopians were forced to go. At the same time a large number who had not participated in Addis Ababa's rule were allowed to stay. Some of those who were expelled had worked in Eritrea all their lives; they knew no other home. One Ethiopian complained: 'The Eritrean soldiers told us we were strangers.

But I was born in Eritrea like everyone else in my family.' Many were forbidden from taking their possessions with them when they left, and some had to abandon houses, businesses and cars.

The deportees included a significant number of Eritrean born women and children who had married or cohabited with Ethiopian civil servants and soldiers. 'Collaborators' of this kind were considered traitors. Even those who were not expelled suffered social ostracism. The newly installed Ethiopian government neither complained nor retaliated. Around half a million Eritreans who had lived in Ethiopia for generations were allowed to remain in the country. Reportedly, the Eritrean community in Addis Ababa had been one of the most reliable sources of intelligence for the Tigrayans and their allies.

The Ethiopian victory presented its own problems for the new rulers in Addis Ababa. Many Ethiopians, watching the Eritrean forces marching into their capital alongside the Tigrayans, assumed that the TPLF was in the EPLF's pocket. This was particularly strongly felt among the Amhara, whom the Tigrayans had displaced from power. They whispered that Meles Zenawi was too pro-Eritrean in his policies. This proved to be a liability for Ethiopia's new leader. Meles was accused of either failing to be robust enough in his defence of his country's interests, or—from the perspective of the TPLF—insufficiently strong in prosecuting policies that favoured his home region of Tigray.

The question of secession, referred to above, also served to drive the movements apart, since their views of administration were diametrically opposed. The new Ethiopian government reformed the state along ethnic lines. The constitution of 1995 allowed for 'a voluntary union of the nationalities of Ethiopia' and included the right to secession. It was the position the EPLF had rejected years earlier. By contrast, the Eritreans built on their vision of their country as a product of colonialism, and opted for a unitary state. They opposed any notion that the state should be ethnically defined. In practice neither government brooked much dissent. Political parties, other than the People's Front for Democracy and Justice—the successor to the EPLF—were not permitted in Eritrea. Some Ethiopian political parties were tolerated, but tightly controlled and frequently repressed.

Despite these tensions the outward signs were that all was well between Addis Ababa and Asmara. Government delegations came and went, and life proceeded as normal. Yet relations between the governments of Ethiopia and Eritrea were not put upon the kind of solid footing that would withstand the strains of office. Part of the problem was that Eritrea achieved de facto independence in May 1991, but this was not formalised until the referendum of May 1993. In the interim there were few official channels of communication. Even after 1993 the leaderships of the two victorious movements continued to treat relations between the two countries as if they were relations between liberation movements. Sometimes they reverted to personal contacts. This may have been because both sides distrusted the institutions they inherited, or because as fighters they had no experience of governmental structures. Hence the bureaucratic infrastructure that should support interstate relations was either not established or else sidelined. If President Isaias had a serious issue that he wished to raise concerning Ethiopia he simply contacted Prime Minister Meles Zenawi, and vice versa. The institutional checks and balances that might have served as restraining influences on both leaders in democratic states were either poorly developed or absent.

This undermined relations between the states in two crucial ways. Firstly, it left plenty of scope for misinterpretations and recriminations. Secondly, it meant that if the relationships between individuals broke down, there were no official structures to fall back upon. Personal relationships and personal histories became entangled with state relations. Even when committees were established, they operated with such informality that when challenged by the critical events that led to the border war, they failed to function effectively.

While the Eritreans and Tigrayans were coming to grips with the administration of their countries, troubling events were taking place along their border. After 1993 a series of localised, small-scale disputes broke out in a number of locations. These were the sorts of conflicts that flare up along any ill-defined border that is straddled by farming communities. Frequently these happened during the ploughing season, as farmers clashed over the exact boundaries of their fields. In earlier times village elders would have sorted out such incidents, for in reality these were 'intra-village' disputes, rather than cross border conflicts. Traditional approaches to conflict-resolution were well-established means of reducing tension. But since 1991 these methods had largely been abandoned along the border. They had been replaced by government to government, or even party to party, meetings between EPLF and TPLF officials. Low-level discussions were held between local officials in an attempt to resolve these matters, but to little avail. In 1992 Eritrea's representative in Ethiopia, Haile Menkerios, warned President Isaias of the need to settle the border but he was rebuffed. A senior adviser to the president, Yemane Gebreab, is quoted as telling Haile that he was 'obsessed with the border issue.' With the dignity of a diplomat Haile replied that he would not raise it again, but warned that unless the issue was addressed it would lead to bloodshed.

Discussions continued, without resolving the question. Following a more serious clash over the Bada area of southern Eritrea, President Isaias Afwerki finally wrote to Prime Minister Meles Zenawi on 25 August 1997, proposing that a Joint Border Commission be established at governmental level. Ethiopia presented a rather different picture of these events, maintaining that the initiative for establishing the Commission came from its side, following a deterioration in relations 'as a consequence of economic issues'.

The first meeting of the Commission took place in Asmara on 13 November 1997. The Eritrean side evidently pressed for a speedy resolution of the border issue, given the deteriorating situation on the ground. According to Ethiopia, a common understanding was reached at the meeting:

- To assign to a technical sub-committee drawn from both countries to examine the border question and to report to the commission to be formed.

- That each party should declare to the other side the list of its members to be represented in the sub-committee.

- That both sides respect the status quo and take measures to alleviate impending border disputes until such time that a lasting solution is attained.

Despite this no further meeting took place until 8 May 1998, with the Eritreans blaming Ethiopian procrastination for the delay.

In the meantime an apparently minor, unrelated event occurred that convinced the Eritreans that the Tigrayans were up to no good. The German government aid agency (the GTZ) operated in three regions of Ethiopia. Early in 1997 the Regional Education Board of Tigray approached the GTZ. They were asked to help fund the printing of a new map of Tigray for distribution to primary schools. The GTZ agreed and printed 1,000 maps with the agency's logo. The map turned out to be deeply controversial, for Eritreans discovered that it portrayed the border in a completely new light. Several areas that had been the subject of the heated discussions between the two countries were now shown as being part of Tigray. Eritreans saw this as proof positive of the hostile intentions of the Tigrayans. It was interpreted as the product of a long held TPLF vision of a 'Greater

Tigray' encompassing all Tigrinya speakers, as outlined in the TPLF manifesto of 1976.

It was against this background that a high level Eritrean delegation left Asmara on 7 May 1998 for a meeting of the Border Commission the following day. Led by Defence Minister Sebhat Efrem, it was en route to Addis Ababa when an incident occurred at the border village of Badme. At first the clash was apparently not regarded as particularly serious, and the Commission's discussions proceeded according to plan. Both sides claim the meeting on the 8th went well. According to the Ethiopians it was agreed that two members of the Commission would meet in Asmara in a month's time to hammer out an agreement and report back to the larger group. They say that it was further accepted that Eritrean armed units that had crossed into Ethiopian territory since 6 May would return to Eritrea and that the status quo ante would prevail until a final agreement had been reached. When the meeting ended the Commission agreed to meet at 10:00 a.m. the following morning, but when the Ethiopians arrived to pick up their guests they discovered that the Eritreans had checked out of their hotel, and flown back to Asmara. In Ethiopian eyes this was a clear indication of a lack of good faith on the part of their guests; as was the rapid appearance of Eritrean armoured units in Badme.

Economics also helped to sour relations between the two states. Open animosity over bilateral trade relations surfaced in late 1997 following Eritrea's introduction of its new currency, the Nakfa. While apparently not a causal factor in the immediate crisis of mid-May, the new currency and ensuing dispute over trade relations had three consequences.

Firstly, the introduction of the Nakfa necessitated a clear delineation of the border from mid-1997 in order to regulate cross-border trade, taxation and foreign exchange flows. Secondly, the new currency prompted a dispute in late 1997 over the precise nature of post-Nakfa trade relations between Eritrea and Ethiopia, tarnishing relations between the two administrations. Thirdly, friction was exacerbated as the currency and trade dispute severely disrupted the flow of goods, remittances and labourers across the border, generating new political tensions between the governments. The currencies—the Nakfa and the Birr—were agreed to be equivalent and interchangeable. These economic factors combined to rekindle old animosities between the ruling groups of both countries, eroding their willingness to compromise or negotiate over disagreements.

In December 1997 a de-facto, partial trade embargo was applied, largely at Asmara's instigation, following the dispute over the introduction of Eritrea's new currency. Nevertheless, normal air, road and telecommunications links remained open. It was only after the fighting at Badme, in mid-May 1998, that a complete rupture took place, as the Ethiopian authorities suspended all trade links and halted the use of the ports of Massawa and Assab for foreign trade.

A number of factors in this complex relationship can be described as cultural. One related to a question of perception. The EPLF had given training and succour to the TPLF in its early stages, and tended to treat the movement as its 'younger brother'. Ordinary Tigrayans, not involved in the politics of the Fronts, also felt patronised and looked down on by Eritreans. They had for years taken low paid, low status jobs in Eritrea, as casual labourers and domestic servants, for example. Tigrayans were denigrated as '*agame*'. The term refers to a district of Tigray from which many migrants came, but it was used to imply that they were uncouth peasants. Most Tigrayan men working in Eritrea were hired as labourers. Some got work slaughtering farm animals, while others took up jobs as woodcutters, potters and shepherds. Women were hired as waitresses, housemaids and washer-women. On the other hand educated Eritreans, who had saved from their earnings, used their skills and capital to buy into or build up businesses in Ethiopia. Class, privilege, snobbery and envy were unspoken elements that ate away at the relationship between the Fronts.

A further issue was communications. Ethiopians and Eritreans are reserved by nature. This trait was exacerbated by the need for secrecy when conducting a campaign of guerrilla warfare. It became ingrained in both movements during the long years of fighting the Ethiopian government. Sometimes this was required by the circumstances of the conflict. Eritreans forbade all discussion of family and origins, partly to ensure that their members concentrated entirely on the fight for independence. It was also vital given that the entire Eritrean population numbered around just three million people. The EPLF feared infiltration to extract information. They were fighting a far stronger enemy, with intelligence support first from the CIA and then later from the Soviet and East German security agencies. There was also a concern that—given the small population—many might have known each other personally. Personal information might endanger families still living behind enemy lines. Understandable as these fears might have been during the war, these practices were so engrained that they were not abandoned even after the movement took the capital in 1991. While this cult of confidentiality may have served both movements well during the years of turmoil, it allowed for misunderstandings to multiply and for rumour to replace open discussions that might have resolved genuine differences.

Finally there was the machismo that was an accretion of the long years of struggle. Both movements and both leaderships had been hardened by battle and suffered from what might be termed a 'Spartan complex'. Anything less than a steely will was seen as a sign of weakness. They had developed a resolution that saw them through the most difficult of times. The Fronts inculcated in their members a determination to press ahead, no matter the cost. This too militated against resolving differences through compromise.

None of these issues were insurmountable. Given time and patience they could, and probably would, have been resolved. But instead of eliminating their differences after they came to power in 1991 they had been allowed to accumulate.

Some analysts who knew both Fronts well warned that there could be trouble in store. John Young—who wrote an influential history of the TPLF—predicted in 1996 that 'political differences between the TPLF and the EPLF during their years of struggle will be reflected in their present and future relations, and as a result they may be far more problematic than is generally imagined.' He was proved tragically correct.

The border war

By mid-1998 old differences, compounded by fresh divisions and irritations, had turned cautious allies into adversaries. All that was required was a spark to set off hostilities. The small-scale land disputes along the undemarcated frontier had been allowed to fester. The spark that led to the conflagration came on 6 May 1998—with gunshots at the border village of Badme. Home to between 3,500 and 5,000 farmers and herders, it was a location so insignificant that few in either capital had ever heard of it. Exactly what transpired in that initial clash is not entirely clear, but the situation was certainly tense even before the first bullet was fired. As the Ethiopian prime minister, Meles Zenawi, put it later, the incident was like: 'Sarajevo, 1914. It was an accident waiting to happen.'

On the day the first shots were fired an Eritrean patrol entered an Ethiopian-administered area on the Badme Plain. They refused to leave their weapons on the outskirts of the village and a clash ensued in which at least one Eritrean was killed. The Eritrean military were outraged. A BBC reporter in Asmara recounted, 'As one general told me, banging his fist on the desk in his office: "To die on the battlefield is one thing, there is honour, but to be killed in cold blood is completely unacceptable. They must be punished."' At this point both sides completely overplayed their hands. Two Eritrean infantry brigades, complete with artillery and tank support, forced the Ethiopians out of Badme. A day later the Ethiopian Parliament declared war. The conflict, fought over the next two years, cost around 100,000 lives and resulted in a million civilians being displaced.

As is almost invariably the case in conflicts, each side blamed the other for triggering the outbreak of war. Both countries put forward incompatible demands that remained essentially unchanged throughout the dispute. Ethiopia called for Eritrea's unconditional withdrawal, since it asserted that Badme was part of its sovereign territory. Eritrea demanded a demilitarisation of the area and arbitration, since it believed the ownership of Badme was under dispute. Despite months of fruitless diplomacy by the United States and Rwanda (which had close links with both sides) this stalemate was only finally broken by events on the battlefield.

In the meantime both sides mobilised for war. Positions along the border were reinforced, with reports of up to 200,000 soldiers being deployed. There were patriotic appeals from Addis Ababa to the farmers in Tigray, requesting that they provide the Ethiopian army with food. In the event the first major round of fighting, which took place between 22 May and 11 June 1998, was brief and bloody, and largely confined to clashes close to the border. Both countries also began massive international purchases of arms and ammunition.

At first Ethiopian troops, caught unprepared for the Eritrean onslaught, were forced onto the defensive. The Eritrean airforce bombed the Tigrean regional capital of Mekele and the town of Adigrat. During an air-raid on Mekele on 5 June an elementary school was hit and 51 civilians were killed and 132 wounded, arousing enormous anger across Ethiopia. While this fighting was taking place the international community attempted to intervene. On 15 May 1998, just two days after the conflict became public, President Hassan Gouled Aptidon of Djibouti arrived in Addis Ababa offering to mediate between the combatants. Isaias rejected the offer in a characteristically brusque fashion.

Two days later the United States Assistant Secretary of State for African Affairs, Susan Rice, flew into the Ethiopian capital on a joint mediation mission with Rwandan prime minister, Paul Kagame. From the beginning of the war there was an intense and continuing diplomatic engagement with the problem. A formal proposal for a full cease-fire, with an indication of how the conflict might be resolved, was actually worked out remarkably rapidly by the United States and Rwanda, and presented to both countries on 30 and 31 May:

The US.—Rwandan recommendations are summarised as follows:

1) Both parties should commit themselves to the following principles: resolving this and any other dispute between them by peaceful means; renouncing force as a means of imposing solutions; agreeing to undertake measures to reduce current tensions; and seeking the final disposition of their common border, on the basis of established colonial treaties and international law applicable to such treaties.

2) To reduce current tensions, and without prejudice to the territorial claims of either party; a small observer mission should be deployed to Badme; Eritrean forces should redeploy from Badme to positions held before May 6, 1998; the previous civilian administration should return; and there should be an investigation into the events of May 6, 1998.

3) To achieve lasting resolution of the underlying border dispute, both parties should agree to the swift and binding delimitation and

demarcation of the Eritrea-Ethiopian border. Border delimitation should be determined on the basis of established colonial treaties and international law applicable to such treaties, and the delimitation and demarcation process should be completed by a qualified technical team as soon as possible. The demarcated border should be accepted and adhered to by both parties, and, upon completion of demarcation, the legitimate authorities assume jurisdiction over their respective sovereign territories.

4) Both parties should demilitarise the entire common border as soon as possible.

This text was then taken up and worked on intensively by the Organisation of African Unity and became what was known as the 'Framework Agreement.' What is remarkable about this draft is that although it was presented to both parties less than a month after the outbreak of hostilities, it contained most of the key elements to be found in the final peace treaty that was signed in Algiers two and a half years later. These include the idea that an international mission should be placed along the border, that Eritrea should withdraw its forces to the areas it held before 6 May, and that the border should be delimited on the basis of colonial treaties and international law.

Ethiopia was broadly satisfied with the US-Rwandan proposals and declared as much, stating that they were 'in-line in substance with the position of the Ethiopian Government on the crisis.' Eritrea, on the other hand, was not at all happy with the plan. They refused to withdraw their forces from Badme, since this would leave the disputed town in Ethiopian hands. Privately they complained bitterly that the Americans under Susan Rice had attempted to 'bounce' them into accepting the proposals, copies of which were apparently released to the press before Asmara had even had sight of them. President Isaias had little time for Rice. He had even less time for her associate, Gayle Smith, who had previously represented the TPLF in the United States.

THE THORNY RELATIONSHIP WITH ETHIOPIA

What followed was a war that surpassed all other African conflicts since the Second World War. The two countries mobilised more than half a million troops and spent hundreds of millions of dollars on the best military equipment they could lay their hands on. Modern jet fighters, heavy artillery and tanks were deployed; vast networks of trenches were dug and minefields were laid. The fighting ranged from massed troop charges to probing raids.

Three rounds of fighting took place, with Ethiopia gradually gaining the upper hand. In the end its superior manpower, drawn from its far larger population (some 60 million as opposed to Eritrea's 4 million) combined with its greater access to Soviet and East European military hardware, took its toll on the Eritrean armed forces. A third round of fighting, in May 2000, saw Ethiopian troops break through in the Western lowlands of Eritrea. The Eritrean forces were rapidly outflanked and lost most of the fertile Gash-Barka region, including the cities of Agordat and Barentu. The Eritreans retreated into the rugged mountains around the town of Keren, which they managed to hold. In the centre the Eritreans suffered further reverses, while Ethiopian forces came close to taking the eastern port of Assab. The Eritrean capital Asmara and the port of Massawa were bombed.

Finally, on 14 June 2000, with Ethiopia controlling nearly a quarter of Eritrean territory, the war came to a halt. Four days later both sides agreed to an OAU proposal for a cessation of hostilities and the establishment of a 25-kilometre wide, temporary security zone running inside Eritrea. A United Nations peacekeeping force—the United Nations Mission to Ethiopia and Eritrea, or UNMEE—would patrol this zone and ensure that neither side breached the peace, while a permanent peace was brokered. Talks to find a durable end to the war had opened in Algiers on 30 May. The meeting was convened by the Organisation of African Unity and attended by Anthony Lake representing the US and Rino

Serri representing the European Union. Despite vitriolic comments from each side about the other, progress was remarkably swift. It soon became clear that Ethiopia's victories on the battlefield had overcome Eritrean intransigence. On 1 June Ethiopian Prime Minister Meles Zenawi announced the war was over, although some sporadic fighting continued around Assab for about a week. Finally, on 18 June, both sides formally agreed to end their two year old conflict.

Indirect talks continued to flesh out the agreement, focussing on technical issues surrounding the role of the peacekeepers and their mandate. Both countries maintained large armies along the border, with as many as 200,000 troops on each side facing each other in trenches that were as little as 50 metres apart in some areas. Despite this, the cease-fire held.

On 14 September 2000 the first UN military observers arrived in Addis Ababa and Asmara. In November the UNMEE force commander, Major General Patrick Cammaert, arrived in Asmara to begin his assignment. A few days later he was joined in the region by the UN Secretary General's special representative, Legwaila Joseph Legwaila, who headed the mission's political arm. Finally, on 12 December 2000 the war was formally concluded when Ethiopian Prime Minister Meles Zenawi and Eritrean President Isaias Afwerki signed an agreement in Algiers to bring the war to an end. The Algiers peace agreement allowed for the establishment of a number of independent commissions to demarcate the border, examine the claims of both sides for damages they had suffered and investigate the causes of the war. The International Committee of the Red Cross was given the responsibility for the repatriation of prisoners of war and internees. [See Appendix 3]

After signing the agreement President Isaias said he hoped that: 'The chapter of cycles of conflicts and hatred can be closed... [we can now] forget the past and look into a future of peace and hope for our two brother peoples'. Prime Minister Meles was not as optimistic, saying that the peace agreement would not in itself bring about normal relations with Eritrea. That, he warned, would require a change of government. On this depressing note one of Africa's bloodiest and bitterest wars drew to a close. The region could look forward to the embrace of a frosty peace.

With the war at an end and international organisations attempting to come to grips with the devastation that had been left behind, it was time to count the cost.

Tens of thousands of soldiers had been killed and wounded. Their exact number will probably never be known. In early 2001 Ethiopian officials began informing families individually of the deaths of their relatives. Each family received a lump sum of six months salary (of around $300) and a small pension. There was no announcement of the overall death toll, but officials privately accept that between 30,000 and 60,000 were killed. Eritrea waited until Martyr's Day 2003—20 June, the day on which it commemorates the sacrifice of its fighters during its war of independence—to announce that it had lost 19,000 in the conflict. There is no independent verification of this figure and no announcement of the numbers of wounded or disabled on either side. But at least families could now grieve for those they had lost. Unofficial estimates of the dead varied between 100,000 and 300,000.

Vast numbers of Ethiopians and Eritreans had been displaced by the fighting. The Ethiopian offensive of May 2000 forced more than a million Eritreans—nearly a third of the population—to flee. Ethiopia too had its share of displaced, although the numbers concerned were considerably lower, since Eritrean troops had not penetrated much beyond their mutual border. Around 315,000 Ethiopians had to leave their homes, mostly in the Tigray region around border towns like Zalambessa. A smaller number (approximately 29,000) were displaced in the Afar region. Death, injury and the flight of civilians are tragic but all too predictable aspects of most modern conflicts. What characterised the Ethiopia—Eritrea war was the accompanying expulsion of the citizens of the opposing country. Not that all these 'foreigners' were expelled, but a terrible price was exacted on ordinary people for the 'sins' of governments over whom they had no control.

In June 1998 Ethiopia set in motion a campaign against Eritrean civilians inside its territory. They were stripped of their Ethiopian citizenship, rounded up, often in the dead of night and bussed across the border. Families were broken up, children separated from their mothers. Travel papers were stamped: 'Expelled, never to return.' Many of those who were treated in this way had never been to Eritrea and knew no home other than Ethiopia. In all, about 75,000 people were deported.

Eritrea promised at the outbreak of war that its remaining Ethiopian residents would not be penalised and at first this was broadly observed. From August 1998 until January 1999 some 21,000 Ethiopians left Eritrea voluntarily, as work at the port of Assab dried up. As the war grew in intensity the hostility towards Ethiopians living in Eritrea increased. Individuals were beaten up and there were reports of rape after major battles. The Eritrean authorities initiated a programme of internment. Following the major Ethiopian offensive in May 2000, Ethiopians were forced to register with local authorities in preparation for repatriation, and shortly afterwards 7,500 were put across the border. The expulsions continued even after the Algiers peace agreement of December 2000; by March 2003 UNICEF estimated that around 60,000 Ethiopians expelled from Eritrea were living in difficult circumstances in Tigray.

Aftermath of the war

The Algiers peace agreement was designed not only to end the war but also to regulate the post-war relationship between

Ethiopia and Eritrea. It incorporated a number of earlier under-takings entered into by both sides, including the Agreement on the Cessation of Hostilities, and the earlier Framework Agreement and the Modalities for its Implementation, endorsed by the OAU summit, July 1999. The Algiers agreement estab-lished, or called on, four separate organisations to assist Ethiopia and Eritrea to move from war to peace. Each was assigned a specific task, with a separate system of reporting. The fifth was the United Nations peacekeeping mission, which had already been envisaged in the Cessation of Hostilities Agreement of 18 June 2000.

The Red Cross ensured the safe repatriation of prisoners; the OAU was asked to investigate the causes of the war; the border itself would be designated by a Boundary Commission working in the Hague and UNMEE would guarantee the peace with its 4,200 strong force patrolling the border. It was a gold-plated peace agreement, drawn up with the best of intentions by skilled negotiators from across the globe. But it came up against the intransigence of both parties. Their unwillingness to compromise for the common good, together with an unwillingness of the international community to enforce the agreement, left Eritrea and Ethiopia locked into a bitter, armed truce. They have con-fronted each other since 2000 in a situation which can be described as 'no war–no peace.'

The International Committee of the Red Cross performed its role with great efficiency. Working quietly behind the scenes it managed to return the last prisoners of war by the end of 2002: 2,067 Eritreans and 1,067 Ethiopians. In addition the Red Cross assisted in the repatriation of 5,055 Ethiopian and 1,086 Eritrean civilian internees. The Organisation of African Unity conducted its own enquiry into the war, but this has never seen the light of day. In July 2003 it was declared simply that its publication was deemed 'not conducive' to the peace process.

The Boundary Commission to establish the border, and a parallel Claims Commission to assess damages, were established at the Permanent Court of Arbitration in the Hague. The Boundary Commission was headed by one of the most eminent legal authorities on borders and boundary disputes, Sir Elihu Lauterpacht. The five-man commission took evidence from both parties, allowed each side to respond to the other and finally published its binding decision on the border on 13 April 2002. The 125-page adjudication, with accompanying maps, drew on treaties drawn up between Ethiopia and Italy of 1900, 1902 and 1908. The reasoning behind their adjudication was long and complex, but turned on two specific points: the provisions of the treaties and whether either party had established by administration a claim so strong that it superseded the provisions contained in those treaties.

The Boundary Commission decided that the position of the critical Western portion of the border, which covered the town of Badme, rested on one specific portion of the 1902 treaty (to which Britain was also a party since it related to the frontier between Eritrea and Sudan). Point three of this text indicated that part of the Ethiopia—Eritrea border would be drawn so that 'the Canama [sic.] tribe belong to Eritrea.' From this single phrase the Commission decided that the village was rightly Eritrean. The Commission went on to examine Ethiopia's claim that it had administered the Badme area for such a long time that it had won effective title to the area, even if it had not been awarded the town by treaty. Having looked at evidence like the collection of taxes, the establishment of an elementary school and the destruction of incense trees the Commission concluded that: 'The Commission does not find in them evidence of administration of the area sufficiently clear in location, substantial in scope or extensive in time to displace the title of Eritrea that had crystallized as of 1935.'

That appeared to be clear enough. Certainly the legal team that drew it up thought they had made their decision crystal clear. Unfortunately the Commission did not indicate the location of Badme on the maps that accompanied the decision. Instead they gave the co-ordinates of the line along which the border would run. Exactly why Badme was not shown on the maps is open to speculation. There is no doubt that a great deal rested on the location of this village, since whoever had legitimate title to it could justifiably claim that they had only been defending their own sovereign territory when the initial conflict erupted. It may be that the jurists thought it would be too controversial to rub Ethiopia's nose in this uncomfortable fact. In taking this decision they unwittingly unleashed a controversy that has yet to be resolved.

Both countries had their own legal teams at the Hague when the decision was given. So too were observers from the United Nations and the Organisation of African Unity. According to a senior UN official the observers were given very little time to study the lengthy judgement. One of the OAU staff in the Hague had been instructed to communicate with the secretary general of the OAU, Omara Essy, on the outcome as soon as possible. So within an hour of it being made public an email was sent to OAU headquarters outlining the ruling. The first point reads as follows:

'1. Western Sector. Delimitation line follows claim of Eritrea i.e. from common border with Sudan, follows Mereb river down to Setit point 6 and straight to Mai Ambessa, point 9. This confirms the Colonial boundary and Ethiopia retains Badme.'

The result was electric. The Ethiopian foreign minister, Seyoum Mesfin, called a press conference to announce the good news. This is from the official transcript of that conference made by the United Nations:

Rarely are press conferences punctuated by applause but at Saturday's press conference given by Minister of Foreign Affairs, Ethiopian journalists punched fists in the air and applauded Seyoum Mesfin as he told them that all the government's territorial demands had been met... Minister Seyoum's demeanor when he finally took the high table was one of wry vindication... After the press conference journalists were in jubilant mood and treated to food and drinks in a party atmosphere. In town people were glued to radio sets and televisions listening to the minister's statement.

On the question of Badme, the foreign minister told the journalists: 'The rule of law has prevailed over the rule of jungle. This decision has rejected any attempt by Eritrea to get reward for its aggression. This decision was fair and legal. Badme and its surroundings which Eritrea invaded and occupied in May 1998 on the basis of its false claims, it's now been decided by the Commission that Badme and its surroundings belong to Ethiopia.' The journalists stood and cheered. Eritrea took the news more coolly, putting out a statement attacking the 'flowery and bombastic statements' that were issued by Ethiopia and declaring simply that 'it is the Eritrean people who have emerged victorious.'

So who was right? Within a few hours a member of the UN staff tipped me off that the Ethiopian interpretation was inaccurate. He explained that when the UN had consulted its maps, using the co-ordinates supplied by the Boundary Commission, it was clear that Badme was just inside Eritrea. When I looked at the decision carefully it became clear that Seyoum Mesfin's interpretation of the text was indeed incorrect. The location of the border had been drawn so that both Ethiopia and Eritrea won and lost certain areas that they had previously considered their own. But on the critical question of Badme, which had triggered the war, the ruling was clear: the village had been awarded to Eritrea. Jubilation in Addis Ababa turned to disbelief and then to fury. Ethiopia sent its information minister to London to see senior BBC managers to try to get my report withdrawn, but the BBC refused. Soon academics backed my interpretation of the ruling. It was clear that

Eritrea had indeed been awarded Badme, even though other areas of the frontier were decided in Ethiopia's favour.

Whatever outsiders felt about the judgement the two parties reacted rapidly. Eritrea, although unhappy about aspects of the ruling, other than Badme, decided it had won a moral victory and asked for its speedy implementation. Ethiopia, on the other hand, was unwilling to accept the outcome and submitted a lengthy comment on the Commission's decision in January 2003, asking for the ruling to be re-considered. A statement from the Foreign Ministry said, 'the Commission made it known that its decision would be based not on the colonial treaty but the subsequent practice of the parties. It also affirmed in its decision that the boundary co-ordinates are provisional, and that they would only be final and binding after verification on the ground.' Ethiopia argued that to implement the ruling without taking into account the impact on farmers and villages, whose lands would be divided by the border, would impose an unacceptable human cost on those concerned.

The normally rather reticent Boundary Commission defended itself robustly against these charges. It pointed out that the decision had been based firmly on the treaties and that it had been given no scope for varying the co-ordinates, except for purely technical reasons. It was specifically precluded from taking into account the human suffering that any of its decisions precipitated by the terms of the Agreement signed by both countries. Article 4 (2) of the Algiers Agreement stated that: 'The Commission shall not have the power to make decisions *ex aequo et bono*.' In other words, that it should rule solely on the legal merits of the case, without considering whether it was fair or equitable. The Commission was particularly tart about the question of Badme, saying that the Ethiopian evidence to it had been 'inconsistent' about its location and that some of the Ethiopian maps presented to it also had Badme within Eritrea. As a result the Commission found in Eritrea's favour: 'This conclusion followed from the inadequacy of Ethiopia's evidence.'

The statement was not well received in Addis Ababa, which simply dug in its heels. Under intense pressure from his own political party, Prime Minister Meles appealed informally to the international community for time and understanding. Asmara continued to insist that demarcation proceed without delay, urging the United Nations to be 'more courageous' and expressing its 'frustration and impatience.' The head of UNMEE, Legwaila Joseph Legwaila, was left warning that peace in the region would be endangered, unless both sides started talking to each other. 'The status quo, that is non-communication between the two governments, complicates the situation. When you don't talk to each other, misunderstandings can lead to conflict.' Declaring that there was a danger of a stalemate, Mr Legwaila said, 'It is not the intention of the UN Security Council to watch and see this become another Cyprus.' He went on to point out that without demarcation the peace that the UN had managed to maintain would be meaningless.

Mr Legwaila's appeals fell on deaf ears. Neither side was prepared to talk to the other. On 9 September 2003 matters took a turn for the worse when Prime Minister Meles wrote to the UN Secretary General expressing open criticism of the Boundary Commission's work. This was followed by a further letter to the Security Council from Ethiopia on 22 September urging it to salvage the peace process, and declaring that the Boundary Commission was in a 'terminal crisis.' The three page letter called on the UN body to 'set up an alternative mechanism to demarcate the contested parts of the boundary.' 'It is unimaginable for the Ethiopian people to accept such a blatant miscarriage of justice,' warned Prime Minister Meles.

The Boundary Commission responded forcefully to this attack. Sir Elihu Lauterpacht rejected any notion of a terminal crisis:

The Commission does not accept that assessment: there is no 'crisis', terminal or otherwise, which cannot be cured by Ethiopia's compliance with its obligations under the Algiers Agreement, in particular its obligations to treat the Commission's delimitation determination as 'final and binding' (Article 4.15) and 'to cooperate with the Commission, its experts and other staff in all respects during the process of... demarcation' (Article 4.14).

Sir Elihu went on to point out that Ethiopia's proposal to establish an alternative mechanism to demarcate the contested parts of the border was a 'repudiation of its repeated acceptance of the Commission's Decision since it was rendered.'

The force of the argument had little impact on the Ethiopian authorities, who had clearly lost face. Unable to get their way, they insisted instead on further discussions with the Eritreans on implementing the Boundary Commission's ruling. Eritrea, believing—probably rightly—that this was simply a manoeuvre to re-open the ruling, rejected any notion of talks. Instead President Isaias insisted that the international community, which had been witnesses to the Algiers Agreement, should fulfil their implied obligation and force Ethiopia to abide by their undertaking to regard the Commission's ruling as 'final and binding.'

On 25 November 2014 Meles Zenawi proposed to the Ethiopian parliament that a fresh attempt should be made to end the stalemate. He put forward a five-point offer, which the parliament adopted:

1. Resolve the dispute between Ethiopia and Eritrea only and only through peaceful means.
2. Resolve the root causes of the conflict through dialogue with the view to normalising relations between the two countries.
3. Ethiopia accepts, in principle, the Ethiopia-Eritrea Boundary Commission decision.
4. Ethiopia agrees to pay its dues to the Ethiopia-Eritrea Boundary Commission and to appoint field liaison officers.

5. Start dialogue immediately with the view to implementing the Ethiopia-Eritrea Boundary Commission's decision in a manner consistent with the promotion of sustainable peace and brotherly ties between the two peoples.

Had there been sufficient goodwill, this offer might have resolved the issue, but there was not. Ethiopia's suggestion that there be an immediate 'dialogue' to implement the Commission's decision ran into the Eritrean insistence that there was really nothing to discuss: all that was required was an unqualified Ethiopian acceptance.

The Eritreans relied on the United States to twist Ethiopia's arm and to enforce compliance with the ruling. Washington may have used diplomatic pressure behind the scenes to try to get Addis Ababa to change its position, but overt pressure was never going to be exerted. Ethiopia was, and remains, too strategically important in the region for America to alienate. The collapse of legitimate authority in Somalia and the growing threat of al-Shabaab and 'Islamic State' in the wider Horn of Africa have meant that Ethiopia is an indispensible ally. No matter how correct the authorities in Asmara might be they were never going to win the wholehearted support of the United States.

Having said this it is also true that President Isaias played his cards extraordinarily badly. He alienated the United Nations peacekeepers by imposing ever-more severe restrictions on their operations. The UN finally terminated UNMEE's mandate in July 2008, since it was no longer fulfilling any useful function. Even the international charities that had been sympathetic to the Eritrean cause were first forced to pay taxes on all their imports—including food and medicines—and then they too were told to leave the country. By comparison, Prime Minister Meles was a model of reasonableness. He worked hard to mend fences with the international community, and with the West in particular. Even though he was in the wrong about Badme and the border demarcation the prime minister was a consummate negotiator and won important diplomatic victories.

What had begun as a minor border skirmish has completely transformed relations between the two neighbours. Ethiopia was left with a large garrison in place along the border and no access to the sea via its traditional ports—Massawa and Assab. The people of Tigray, who have traditionally moved freely across the border to trade and meet family members in Eritrea, have been unable to do so. For Eritrea the consequences have been even more serious. They too lost this social interaction, as well as the revenues from the ports of Massawa and Assab, which had continued to serve Ethiopia after independence in 1991. The Eritrean government felt it had to maintain a vast army on permanent border duties, fearing a fresh conflict. This is not beyond the realms of possibility: indeed, there have been several clashes along the border since peace was declared, the most recent in June 2016, leaving many dead and injured. The military confrontation has drained the political and economic lifeblood out of Eritrea. It has also severely undermined its democracy.

These neighbours—who shared so much in common—have become locked into a vicious cold peace, determined to do all they can to undermine each other without actually resorting to open warfare. There is no way of knowing if either will one day overstep the mark and full-scale war will not resume.

* * *

The conflict with Ethiopia has sometimes been regarded as an issue of little substance. Commentators have dismissed the border war of 1998–2000 as 'two bald men quarrelling over a comb.' This is a trite, vaguely amusing quip, but hardly accurate. The differences between the two major parties—EPLF and TPLF—run very deep indeed. There was a bitter ideological divergence between them that was reinforced by events. This may have seemed relatively insignificant at the time, but divisions became ingrained in the psyches of the leading members of both movements. Differences culminated in the Eritrean decision to close the border to the Tigrayans just when they needed access to Sudan most: at the height of the 1984–85 famine. Hundreds, possibly thousands, died as a result, hence it was hardly surprising that the TPLF regarded it as a 'savage act'. This was hardly the basis for a long-term relationship. Rather, a hostile, conflictual relationship was established which has proved sadly enduring. Both countries have paid a high price in treasure and blood to maintain the 'no-war, no-peace' that now characterises this stalemate.

4

QUARRELLING WITH NEIGHBOURS

The independence of Eritrea in 1993 should have been a moment for celebration for all the countries of the Horn of Africa. It drew a line under thirty years of conflict in the region. For a while the Eritreans apparently went about their business with few quarrels with their neighbours, but this did not last. Soon President Isaias launched a very different policy: one which saw neighbouring states as threats that had to be countered. Perhaps these quarrels were inevitable. After all, Eritrea was a new state, which had to assert its territorial integrity: something that is common to many newly independent nations.

Dan Connell, a long-time observer of Eritrean affairs, put it very well when he wrote that the regime believed that 'the best defence of its borders against hostile acts by neighbouring states or by oppositional groups based in them is the construction of effective insurgent forces that challenge these regimes from within and that will, as a quid pro quo, assist in patrolling Eritrea's borders—effectively acting as buffers.' Eritrea is not alone in adopting this strategy. It has, unfortunately, become the dominant expression of foreign policy across the Horn of

Africa. It is what the British Africanist Lionel Cliffe called 'mutual intervention.'

Eritrean support for these rebel movements is conducted via what the UN describes as a 'small but efficient team of officers' from the National Security Office, the Eritrean military and the ruling party (the PFDJ) 'under the direct supervision of the President's Office. This narrow clique of senior officers, reporting to President Isaias, maintains a network of training centres, camps and other facilities. Their work is led by Brigadier General Te'ame Goitom Kinfu (also known as Wedi Meqelle) who is in charge of Eritrea's External Operations Directorate.'

A squabble over islands

Just two years after formal independence Eritrea had become entangled in a serious quarrel with another small country on the other side of the Red Sea: Yemen. For generations their fishermen had plied these waters. Mostly they fished, sometimes they smuggled goods and transported people. The Red Sea is one of the busiest shipping lanes in the world. It is also dotted with hundreds of islands—some large and many small—which make up the Hanish archipelago. Roughly equidistant between Yemen and Eritrea, it was not clear in which country's territory they fell.

On 20 December 1995 Yemeni President Ali Abdullah Salih was pleased to announce that a German company had submitted an application for a £1 million hotel and scuba diving complex on Greater Hanish island. For President Isaias and the Eritrean leadership this rang alarm bells. The islands were disputed territory and Eritrea was not about to renounce its claims so easily. Telephone calls between the two heads of state failed to resolve the issue. So did a Yemeni deputation sent to Eritrea. Eritrea was willing to refer the matter to the International Court of Justice, but only if all 200 odd islands in the Hanish archipelago were considered, a suggestion that Yemen balked at.

Frustrated by its inability to resolve the matter amicably, Eritrea attacked. Despite having neither a navy nor an airforce it captured Greater Hanish using small craft, taking 95 Yemeni troops captive. At this point the United States and the United Nations intervened before matters got further out of hand. A French diplomat, Francis Gutmann, was appointed and by May 1996 an agreement was reached. The matter was referred to a tribunal established by the Permanent Court of Arbitration. The tribunal worked hard, taking evidence and consulting hundreds of maps dating back many centuries. As the judges put it dryly, they looked at 'more maps of every conceivable period and provenance than have ever been seen before'.

The ruling went almost entirely in Yemen's favour. President Isaias gritted his teeth and accepted the ruling. In itself the loss of almost all the islands beyond Eritrea's 12-mile coastal zone made little difference. The tribunal called on both nations to allow the fishermen of Eritrea and Yemen to continue their historic activities. But it established an important precedent: Eritrea and its government would stand by international treaties and agreements, even when they went against their country's perceived national interests. This was important. When Ethiopia refused to abide by the Algiers treaty that ended their border war and the ruling by the Permanent Court of Arbitration, Eritrea assumed the international community would back its cause. Eritrea looked to the United States for assurance in this regard since Washington had been directly involved in drafting the Algiers treaty, but they were sorely disappointed.

An indication of just how badly President Isaias felt he was treated can be judged from this answer he gave to the *Los Angeles Times* in October 2007:

> The U.S. has come out to openly say that they were on the side of Ethiopia against Eritrea... We believe the U.S. deliberately complicated the process [of demarcating the border in accordance with a 2002 Court

of Arbitration ruling that gave Badme to Eritrea] to delay it and find some opportune moment for reversal. These five years of complications have not come from the regime in Addis. It's come from Washington.

The president's inclination to blame anyone but himself for his country's misfortunes is characteristic of Isaias. At the same time one can feel some sympathy for the frustration of the president and his government, given the way they were treated by the U.S. Eritrea had been persuaded to abide by international judgements over the Hanish islands—now the international community was abandoning it to its fate.

At the same time it is important to understand the exaggerated role President Isaias believed his country should enjoy. At independence he saw Eritrea as the major player in the region. This may seem strange for such a tiny nation, but Isaias really believed Eritrea was pivotal to the future of the Horn of Africa. The EPLF, which had helped its Ethiopian allies in the early days of their rebellion against the emperor, thought of themselves as the 'big brothers' of their Ethiopian colleagues, the TPLF. Unsurprisingly, this was not an opinion shared by Ethiopia's new leader, Meles Zenawi, or the rest of his countrymen. Isaias Afewerki also believed his country's victory was a vindication of the belief that nothing was impossible if there was sufficient will to achieve it. He began to exercise his powers well beyond the Horn of Africa.

One of the earliest indications of Isaias's foreign policy ambitions came in a most unlikely setting: the war that erupted in the Democratic Republic of Congo in 1996. Eritrea had been good friends with the Rwandan government of Paul Kagame. When Kagame decided to overthrow Congolese President Mobutu Sese Sekou by sending in troops in 1996 the Eritreans came to Rwanda's aid. The spark that led to this conflagration was President Mobutu's support for the Hutu troops that had fled to his country following the Rwandan genocide of 1994—

the 'génocidaires'. From their Congolese bases the Hutus prepared to fight their way back into Rwanda. They sent their troops on raiding parties into Rwanda. President Mobutu was incapable, or unwilling, to halt this aggression. It was a situation the newly installed Rwandan government of Paul Kagame was not prepared to tolerate.

By late 1996 matters had come to a head and Rwanda was plotting the overthrow of President Mobutu. A 'Tutsi legion' consisting of troops from Rwanda, Uganda and Burundi moved into the Congo. They were joined by what the scholar Filip Reyntjens referred to as 'Eritrean and Ethiopian mercenaries'. My information is that the Eritreans were not mercenaries hired on three-month contracts but a full battalion of Eritrean government troops. They invaded Congo in support of Laurent Kabila, then a tavern keeper and little-known Congolese rebel. The 'Tutsi legion' marched across the entire width of the Congo, nearly 1,500 kilometres as the crow flies, and much further on foot. It was an extraordinary feat, especially for soldiers who walked the entire distance in gumboots, with little or no logistical support. The toll on the Eritreans was enormous. By the time they reached Kinshasa in the far West of this giant country in May 1997 they were exhausted and starving. Many had died along the way; others were desperately ill. Ultimately these Eritrean troops had to be evacuated from the Congo.

In May 1998 the border war with Ethiopia erupted and all other concerns were put to one side. Eritrea emerged from the war defeated, but when it became plain that Ethiopia would not abide by the Commission's ruling over the border, and that none of the major powers would compel Addis Ababa to comply, President Isaias was furious. Many Eritreans took a similar view: they had trusted the international community and believed they had been betrayed and humiliated. Eritrea decided that it should do what it had during its long fight for independence: fall back on self-reliance and fight for its rights.

War by proxy

The Eritrean government believed that it would only win control of those areas along its border with Ethiopia that they had been awarded if they forced the government in Addis Ababa to comply with the ruling. At the same time they believed that Prime Minister Meles and his associates were weak; after all, it had required Eritrean troops to help put the Tigrayans in power in 1991. In Eritrean eyes their neighbours had undermined their own position by insisting on ethnic federalism. This meant that Ethiopia was divided along ethnic and linguistic lines, with each group having its own regional state—nine in all. From an Eritrean perspective this was madness. Eritreans believed they had overcome ethnic rivalries and established a national identity as they fought for their independence. If they withdrew their support for Meles—so the argument went—the Ethiopian government would fall. To help matters along, Eritrea began supporting opposition movements inside Ethiopia.

Since the Ethiopian government led by the TPLF was an authoritarian regime that brooked little opposition, the Eritreans had no difficulty in finding willing partners. The Somalis, Oromo and Tigrayans all had grievances against the government in Addis Ababa. They sought external bases, weapons and assistance. This was by no means a one-way trade: the Ethiopians were soon doing much the same with dissident Eritrean groups. Nor was Eritrean backing for rebels restricted to those of Ethiopian origin. Asmara armed opposition movements across the Horn, including Djibouti, Somalia and Sudan. When this was brought to the attention of the United Nations the Security Council imposed sanctions against Eritrea for undermining its neighbours. The first sanctions were adopted in 2009 (resolution 1907) and gradually tightened.

In some ways this was surprising, since the Security Council drew on a Monitoring Report drawn up by a team of Somalia experts dated 10 December 2008 (S/2008/769) which concluded that: 'The presence of Ethiopian forces on Somali territory and its support to allied Somali groups continue to be regarded by the Monitoring Group as violations of the arms embargo. Eritrea continues to provide political, financial and military support to armed opposition groups. Yemen remains the most important source of commercial arms transfers to Somalia.' Yet only Eritrea was singled out for sanctions. The Security Council didn't take equivalent measures against Ethiopia. This indicated the vital importance of Ethiopian forces in countering the Somali Islamists of al-Shabaab. It also reflected the fact that Eritrea was seen as a regional bully, having been held to be responsible for another conflict—its border conflict with Djibouti in 2008 (see below).

To complement the Eritrean sanctions, and to monitor their impact, the UN Monitoring Group was required to provide the Security Council with regular reports. Their extensive publications provide a unique insight into the workings of the Eritrean state. The UN monitors worked hard to maintain their independence. They used, wherever possible, verifiable documentary evidence or first hand accounts. However, they have been criticised for relying too heavily on Ethiopian and United States intelligence. This was perhaps unavoidable, since there are few independent sources of information about Eritrea, since President Isaias refuses to allow international news agencies to be based on Eritrean soil and severely restricts the work of international organisations and diplomats.

Somalia

Somalia has been the fiercest proxy battleground on which the conflict between Ethiopia and Eritrea has been played out. For Ethiopia—with its large and restive Somali population in the semi-desert eastern region of the Ogaden—this has been a critical issue. Somalia has a traditional claim to the Somali speakers of the Ogaden, just as it does to much of Djibouti and Northern Kenya. In July 1977 Somali President Siad Barre invaded Ethiopia in an attempt to take the Ogaden by force. It was only with considerable Soviet and Cuban support that the attack was defeated. Ever since, Ethiopian leaders of all political persuasions have maintained a wary eye on Somalia. Strategists in Addis Ababa have pursued an overriding objective: to keep Somalia weak and divided. To that end Ethiopia has armed a variety of Somali movements. In the early 1990s this was done through private channels. From 1996 Ethiopia became directly involved, sending troops into Somalia to crush any forces they saw as a threat to their interests. Weapons supplies were also provided in large quantities to groups singled out by Ethiopia as potential allies.

Some of the Eritrean leadership knew Somalia well, having used it as a friendly base during their long war of independence. Many had carried Somali passports. With Somalia divided between rival warlords following the fall of the Siad Barre government in 1991, the country was wide open to outside influence. Eritreans therefore regarded Somalia as a natural battleground on which to confront Ethiopia during and after the border war of 1998–2000.

As early as 1999 Hussein Aideed, son of a former Somali president, acknowledged that he received three ship-loads of supplies from Eritrea: two of military equipment and one of food. Equipment was also provided by Eritrea by air during 1998 and 1999. This caused considerable American unease, since some of the weapons were designed to bolster groups fighting the Ethiopian government. As Susan Rice, Assistant Secretary of State for African Affairs told a Congressional Hearing on 25 May 1999: 'We are very concerned by credible reports that Eritrea has delivered large quantities of weapons and munitions to self-proclaimed Somali President Hussein Aideed for the use of a violent faction of the Oromo Liberation Front. The [Ogadeni Islamist] terrorist organisation Al-Ittihad may also be an indirect recipient of these arms.'

By 2006 the Eritreans had switched allies and were arming the Union of Islamic Courts, which briefly held power in Mogadishu. Arms and ammunition arrived by dhow at a string of small ports along the Somali coast, while Eritrean planes landed with vehicles and personnel. Shipments of weapons were also recorded via larger vessels. Fighters belonging to the Union of Islamic Courts were sent to Eritrea where they received training. The Eritrean government provided 'advisers' and 'engineers and mine-laying experts' to assist the Courts. They also despatched around 800 Oromo Liberation Front (OLF) fighters who participated in the battles around Baidoa in December before advancing on Mogadishu. At the same time around 1,000 Ogaden National Liberation Front (ONLF) troops went into the Ogaden through central Somalia and were largely responsible for intensified fighting in the Ogaden in 2007–8.

The Eritrean intervention failed. In December 2006 the Courts were defeated by Ethiopian troops who had invaded the country. The Islamists were driven from Mogadishu. Some of the leadership fled to Eritrea, leaving the more hardline fighters to confront the Somali government and Ethiopia. Al-Shabaab grew out of these fighters, beginning a long and bloody guerrilla campaign against the Ethiopians and their Somali allies.

The Eritreans, always keen to maintain a foothold in Somalia, transferred their allegiance to al-Shabaab. When Jendayi Frazer, the US Assistant Secretary of State for African Affairs, visited Somalia in April 2007 she accused Eritrea of fuelling the insurgency in Somalia. 'No insurgency group can survive without support from neighbouring countries,' Ms Frazer told reporters in Nairobi. 'Certainly Eritrea is the country of greatest concern,' she said. But although Eritrea had previously supplied large quantities of arms and ammunition to its Somali allies, it is less clear that this practice was continued with al-Shabaab. The UN Monitors found little hard evidence of weapons supplies. Rather, their reports have repeatedly alleged that Eritrea sent funds to al-Shabaab via trusted intermediaries. The evidence, which takes the form of documentation and witness reports, points to the Eritrean embassy in Nairobi as the key nexus through which the transfers were made. Payments are said to have begun in 2008 and continued over a number of years. As the activities of its Kenyan embassy came under scrutiny, Eritrea is said to have diversified its funding operation to Sudan, South Sudan, Uganda and Yemen.

Ethiopian rebel movements

At least seven armed rebel groups have received Eritrean patronage at various times. This included providing rear bases and training all the way up to planning sophisticated military operations. Most have their roots in a single ethnic group and the most significant groups are:

- The Ogaden National Liberation Front (a Somali movement)
- The Oromo Liberation Front
- Various Afar movements, including the Afar Revolutionary Democratic Unity Front
- The Tigray People's Democratic Movement

To this list of ethnic rebel groups must be added Ginbot Sebat, otherwise referred to as Ginbot 7. Although its support is predominantly from the Amhara, it receives backing from the country's emerging middle class, of various ethnicities. The movement is led by Berhanu Nega, who won 137 of the 138 seats in the 2005 election for Addis Ababa. He was the mayor elect, but was prevented from taking office by the government. When protests erupted the authorities sent their security forces onto the streets of the capital, crushing opposition and imprisoning its leadership.

The Oromo Liberation Front (OLF), representing Ethiopia's largest ethnic group, has been operating in the borderlands between eastern Sudan and western Ethiopia since 1973. The links between the EPLF and the OLF go back to the wars against the Derg. It was with EPLF help that the OLF managed briefly to capture the Ethiopian town of Assossa in 1989. John Young, who has written extensively about rebel movements in Ethiopia and Sudan, says that OLF fighters were infiltrated into the Ethiopian region of Gambella in mid 2002. He claims that seven OLF battalions, each made up of 150–200 fighters, were transported from Eritrea and cites witnesses as reporting that the OLF fighters flew to the Sudanese town of Akobo. They then marched into Gambella and on into western Wellaga—a state with a high Oromo population. Most were apparently wiped out in clashes with Ethiopian government forces. Young also suggests that there have been some attempts to infiltrate OLF forces into Ethiopia via Somalia. None has been very successful.

The OLF, and its Eritrean allies, then changed tactic. They ended mass infiltration and turned to bombings. In so doing they came closest to achieving their goal of striking a serious blow against the Ethiopian authorities. The chosen target was the African Union summit, scheduled for January 2011. Eritrea planned massive bomb attacks on the gathering at a moment when African heads of state were in attendance. The aim was to place explosives at the Ethiopian prime minister's office, the former imperial palace and the Sheraton hotel, at which many leaders were staying. A further blast was planned for the Mercato area—home to Africa's largest open-air market. The plan was designed to 'make Addis Ababa like Baghdad,' according to the UN Monitors. 'If executed as planned, the operation would almost certainly have caused mass civilian casualties, damaged the

Ethiopian economy and disrupted the African Union summit,' they reported.

The UN Monitors outlined how three teams were trained, armed and briefed by Eritrean security. They were smuggled into Ethiopia via neighbouring Djibouti. The man behind the operation was General Te'ame, the head of the External Operations Directorate. These allegations were denied by the Eritrean government, just as they rejected all other reports from the UN Monitors. In the event the OLF operation was disrupted and most of those involved were either killed or captured. But the scale and audacity of the operation underlined just how serious the threat posed by the Eritrean government really was. The UN report concluded that: 'since the Eritrean intelligence apparatus responsible for the African Union summit plot is also active in Kenya, Somalia, the Sudan and Uganda, the level of threat it poses to these other countries must be re-evaluated.'

The Tigray People's Democratic Movement (TPDM—also known by its Tigrinya acronym 'Demhit') was established in 2001. Like other Ethiopian opposition movements, it grew thanks to President Isaias's patronage. The TPDM has been described as the most important Ethiopian opposition group active inside Eritrea with 'a dual function as an Ethiopian armed opposition group and a protector of the [Eritrean] regime.' The rebels had an estimated strength of 4,000 fighters in 2014, many drawn from refugees fleeing from Ethiopia. The group was a real threat to the government of Ethiopia, since it drew its support from the same ethnic group that currently holds power in Addis Ababa. Like other movements it received training and weapons from the Eritrean regime. Some of its forward bases were close to the Ethiopian border and its members were also to be found at important Eritrean military training camps, including the country's main camp for National Service conscripts at Sawa. The Ethiopians did not take the TPDM's threat lightly and in April

2012 Ethiopian troops were reported to have crossed into Eritrea to attack TPDM bases.

The significance of the TPDM was evident during the most significant challenge to President Isaias's hold on power: the 'Forto' army mutiny of 21 February 2013. These events will be described in detail in Chapter 9. There are reports that with the loyalty of his own forces in question, the president relied on the TPDM for security. They were also allegedly deployed later in the same year to round up Eritrean youths in Asmara who had failed to report for military service. In one incident stones were thrown at TPDM fighters, who opened fire. This reliance on foreign forces was deeply resented by the Eritrean population. 'They demanded the identity documents of a friend of mine and [me]', said a resident of the capital. 'When this happened earlier this year there was a riot. People really hate them.'

Until late 2015 the TPDM was a significant threat to the Ethiopian government, but on 13 September the Ethiopian authorities were able to announce—to their evident satisfaction—that Molla Asgedom, the movement's chairman, had led hundreds of his fighters back into the country. The statement claimed this defection was the result of lengthy contacts between the Ethiopian government and the TPDM leadership. 'The Ethiopia Security began to work with Molla and other "patriotic" individuals in the TPDM leadership since well over year [sic], and the goal of the joint operation was to spy on the activities of the Eritrean regime, transfer information to Addis that would help foil military operations from Eritrea, and eventually pull the entire rebel command out of Eritrea', the government said in a press release.

The Reuters newsagency carried this report:

In a statement, the foreign ministry said TPDM leader [Molla] Asgedom and "nearly 800 fighters" crossed to Ethiopia from Sudan on Sunday, having fought their way past Eritrean troops. 'We came to the conclusion that an armed struggle was meaningless,' [Molla] told the state-run Ethiopian Broadcasting Corporation, adding the group had been in contact with Addis Ababa for over a year before deserting.

Footage of a large group of young men in fatigues and wielding AK-47 rifles and grenade launchers while camped in an open field near Ethiopia's border with Sudan was shown on Ethiopian television. 'The government's sole aim was to disintegrate Ethiopia,' Molla said, referring to Eritrea. If these statements accurately represent Molla's views (and he will have been carefully briefed by the Ethiopian government on what to say) then it seems clear that this was a major breach in Eritrean security. How was it possible for them to miss contacts between the TPDM and the Ethiopians for a year?

Ginbot Sebat, which began as a peaceful political movement, took up arms after its suppression by the Ethiopian regime following the May 2005 election. In the crackdown that ensued in November following opposition demonstrations in Addis Ababa, over 300 people were killed and at least 30,000 detained. Although most of the detainees were released in a matter of weeks, the government handed out long prison sentences to a number of opposition leaders. Again, most were released two years later after they petitioned for a pardon. The opposition decided there was little room left for democratic opposition. Meeting in Washington in 2008, Ginbot 7 was formed; the name, 'May 15' in Amharic, commemorates the day of the 2005 election.

Its recruits fall under the direction of Eritrean Colonel Fitsum Yishak (also known as 'Lenin'). Fistum is deputy commander of the External Operations Directorate, working for General Te'ame whose role is to supervise training for regional opposition movements. Te'ame is also directly involved in training of highland Ethiopian armed opposition groups—the TPDM and Ginbot Sebat. Ginbot fighters who crossed into Eritrea received training in the use of weapons and explosives in a camp at Harena, south of the port of Massawa. Some of their members had been recruited as far afield as South Africa, with the Eritrean embassy in Johannesburg issuing them with documents. Once in Asmara they were met by Ginbot Sebat's secretary general, Andargachew Tsige.

Andargachew, who became involved in politics in the early 1970s resisting the former military regime—the Derg—is a British citizen. He arrived in Britain in 1979, settling in London with his family. But he continued to be actively involved in Ethiopian politics, and travelled constantly for Ginbot Sebat. On 23 June 2014 he was in the Yemeni airport at Sana'a in transit between the United Arab Emirates and Eritrea when he was arrested by Yemeni security services. They arranged his abduction to Ethiopia, in whose prisons he has remained ever since. The British government issued a Foreign Office statement expressing their concern for the circumstances of his arrest and appealing for Andargachew not to face the death penalty. The appeals appear to have succeeded, but there is no sign that he will be released and he continues to languish in an Ethiopian jail.

In 2015 several Eritrean backed Ethiopian armed groups formed a united front, bringing together the TPDM and Ginbot Sebat as well as two other smaller movements—the Patriotic Front and Arbegnoch. The new organisation called itself the 'Salvation Front.' Berhanu Nega became the Front's chairman. But bringing these groups under a single umbrella organisation inevitably led to tensions.

The defection of Molla Asgedom, and his TPDM fighters, is reported to have been the result of differences between Molla and Berhanu. Speaking a few days after Molla's defection to Ethiopia, Berhanu denied that 700 fighters had gone with him. 'The betrayal by the General Molla crew did not affect our movement because TPDM still has thousands of other soldiers left in Eritrea,' Berhanu said. The vice-chairman of TPDM, Mekonnen Tesfay, was quoted as supporting Berhanu's assertion that the Ethiopian opposition army inside Eritrea is still powerful. Although the Eritrean authorities will have been smarting at the loss of these troops they have not abandoned their long-held ambition of undermining the Ethiopian government, which is certain to respond in kind. The two countries are locked into a fragile truce in which proxies play a useful part in their ongoing confrontation.

Fighting Djibouti

As if it did not have enough troubles along its southern border with Ethiopia, Eritrea has clashed with its eastern neighbour, Djibouti on several occassions. As with Ethiopia there are reports of a number of preliminary skirmishes in April 1996 when the two countries almost went to war after a Djibouti official accused Eritrea of shelling the town of Ras Doumeira. In 1999 Eritrea accused Djibouti of siding with Ethiopia, while Djibouti blamed its neighbour for supporting Djiboutian rebels and having designs on the Ras Doumeira region.

Differences between Eritrea and Ethiopia remained, but attempts were made to mend fences. President Isaias visited Djibouti in early 2001 and President Ismail Omar Guelleh made a reciprocal visit to Asmara in the early summer of 2001. Ultimately the smouldering differences erupted into conflict. On 10 June 2008 there were clashes along the border. The government of Djibouti issued a statement saying: 'At 6:40pm [15:40 GMT], under the cover of darkness and prayer time, Eritrean troops opened fire on our soldiers. In the face of this attack, our military struck back... As this statement is published, the fighting continues.' Nine Djibouti soldiers were killed in the engagements and more than sixty wounded. A number were taken prisoner. The scale of the Eritrean casualties is unknown. A formal ceasefire was announced on 9 June 2010, but Eritrea did not leave matters there. It began supporting a faction of FRUD—the Front for the Restoration of Unity and Democracy, a rebel movement representing the Afar people against Djibouti's Issa dominated government. The UN published photos of the FRUD leader, Mohamed Kadd'ami, addressing his troops in October 2009 inside Eritrea. The UN Monitors also mentioned that there was a failed plot by al-Shabaab against Djibouti in January 2015, but the UN has chosen not to publish details of what took place and this element of the report remains confidential.

The clash with Djibouti was unlikely to end well for Eritrea. Djibouti hosts French forces and an American military base—the latter the US Africa Command's most important foothold on the continent. In the last resort both would come to the aid of their hosts. China too is in the process of securing a military foothold in Djibouti. Ethiopia has increased its ties with Djibouti, relying on its port since the loss of Assab and Massawa, with the Chinese renewing the railway line from Djibouti port to Addis Ababa. If Eritrea ever really threatened Djibouti's sovereignty it could find itself facing a number of enemies.

* * *

This is only a brief summary of Eritrea's interventions across the region. At times the Eritrean actions represented the legitimate concerns of a new state, as in the dispute with Yemen. At other times they were attempts to continue their proxy war with Ethiopia. In either case the Eritreans behaved in a characteristically robust fashion: diplomacy was never one of President Isaias's strong suits. To pursue these aims the country has been involved in backing a wide range of movements, providing them with arms and ammunition, training and intelligence. Most often this was in an attempt to prosecute its conflict with Ethiopia by other means. Ethiopia has retaliated in kind, backing Eritrean movements attempting to end President Isaias's rule.

Neither strategy appears to have been particularly successful. After more than a decade of such interventions the governments in Addis Ababa and Asmara are both firmly in place. Neither shows any sign of allowing any change in their policies. Attempts by Eritrea to infiltrate men and weapons into Ethiopia have almost invariably ended in failure. The most sophisticated attempt to attack its southern neighbour—the Oromo plan to disrupt the African Union Summit—was unsuccessful. Many Ethiopians have died attempting to pursue the strategy of armed resistance; others languish in Ethiopian jails. Ethiopia has a sophisticated intelligence service that probably shares information with the United States, which relies in turn on Ethiopia to fight Islamist rebels in Somalia and, until January 2016, had an important drone base in the Ethiopian town of Arba Minch. It would also appear that Ethiopian agents have succeeded in infiltrating Ethiopian (and Eritrean) rebel movements. Taken as a whole, Ethiopia has been largely successful in neutralising Eritrea's strategy of destabilising the government in Addis Ababa.

5

FOREIGN FRIENDS

There is an Eritrean myth that goes something like this: 'We fought for our independence for thirty years. No one came to our aid and we relied entirely on ourselves to defeat Ethiopia, which was supported and armed first by the Americans and then the Soviet Union'. From this comes the basic ideological position of the regime, which is summed up in this adage: 'Stand alone, stand proud: we can do it on our own'. It is a worthy sentiment—indeed, when one sees the dependency that has afflicted so many African states it has much to recommend it. However, when taken to extremes any concept can be destructive. Under Isaias Afewerki, self-reliance became an obsession. It is such an all-encompassing ideology that any diversion from it was (and still is) considered to be a grave mistake. It was seen as little short of treason to question the president's authority, for he believed he was the only person who could safely be entrusted with the independence that had been so hard-won over so many years.

Like all ideologies it has a basis in fact. While Ethiopian regimes, from Haile Selassie to the Derg, relied on foreign forces, vast imports of military supplies and the support of expatriate advisers, Eritrea did not. But this does not mean that it had no external support. Significant early steps towards Eritrean liberation were taken in Cairo. The city had long been an important centre for Eritrean Muslims, especially for the generations of Islamic scholars who had received instruction at Cairo's prestigious Al-Azhar Al-Sharif University. Addis Ababa always believed that there was an Egyptian hand behind every Eritrean rebel group. The reason for this was straightforward. Any economic development in Ethiopia was likely to increase the use of the Blue Nile, which is the lifeblood of the Egyptian people. Any reduction in the river's flow is seen as an existential threat, since the country receives almost no rainfall. As the old adage goes: 'Egypt is the Nile and the Nile is Egypt.' Hence Cairo's attempts covertly to maintain Ethiopia in a weakened state by supporting opposition movements. This policy was pursued quietly, but with vigour. It continues to this day, with Addis Ababa locked in disputes with Egypt over the Grand Renaissance Dam, even though this is designed to produce hydo-electricity for Ethiopia, rather than for irrigation.

The ELF, with its mainly Muslim base, had a natural entry into Arab and Muslim society. In December 1960 leaders of the ELF met the Saudi royal family, including King Saud and Crown Prince Faisal, in Riyadh. They were promised support in the United Nations. A senior member of the Eritrean opposition, Woldeyesus Ammar, recalls that a year later the ELF opened the first Eritrean office abroad in Somalia. This was followed in May 1961 by an invitation from Palestinians to present their case before an Islamic Conference held in Jerusalem.

Algeria, Iraq and Syria also provided assistance, at times. The ELF received its first weapons from Syria in 1963 and nineteen Eritreans went for military training in Aleppo. For the next fifteen years Syria backed the ELF. But young members of the movement gradually became disillusioned with the way their organisation behaved. They believed it was not sufficiently radical, and in response established a study circle in the Sudanese town of Kassala to read the works of revolutionary leaders. Among those who participated in the reading group were Isaias Afewerki and his associate Romadan Nur (who later became the EPLF's secretary general).

During the 1960s a number of radical African and Arab leaders came to power and the Eritreans were able to glean some support. Somalia, Algeria, Libya, Iraq and the Palestine Liberation Organisation provided arms and money. In 1967 and 1968 a small group of ELF fighters was sent for training in China, among them Isaias. A further group went to Cuba. These young Eritreans returned home with more than military training: they had a new way of looking at their world. On arriving in Sudan after his time in China, Isaias was struck by how conservative the ELF was. He felt it was failing to reflect the intellectual trends of the 1960s. 'It was the peak of politics in the ELF,' he later recalled. 'The talk of reform was everywhere. Everyone trained in Syria and elsewhere joined hands. There were all sorts of revolutionary ideas. We had high hopes in those days.' The reforms they called for would split the movement, a development that is dealt with in Chapter 5.

Once the split took place the ELF was able to corner most Arab support, while the socialist EPLF found it easier to make links with radical regimes like the People's Republic of South Yemen, which was based in Aden. Some of the first EPLF landings on Eritrean soil took place from dhows laden with weapons that had set off from Aden, to attack Ethiopian controlled oases in the scorching deserts of the Danakil. Training and weapons from the South Yemen had been an important element in their preparations for the attack.

While the links with Communist states like Cuba were useful, they came at a price. This was the Cold War and the United

States was locked in a confrontation with the Soviet Union and its allies. Developing nations were pawns in this global struggle. When officers overthrew the Ethiopian emperor in September 1974 the country moved to the left. Somewhat reluctantly the Soviet Union was drawn into backing Ethiopia's new military regime, the Derg. As war loomed between Ethiopia and Somalia in 1977 the Cubans attempted to head it off. The Somali President, Siad Barre, was determined to try to recapture territory in Ethiopia's vast, dry eastern region that has long been claimed by the Somali people. The Cuban president, Fidel Castro, mediated between the two countries. Ethiopia's leader Mengistu Haile Mariam and Somalia's President Siad Barre met under Castro's guidance in Aden in March, but to no avail. In July the Somalis mounted a massive attack with 70,000 troops. They forced Ethiopian forces to retreat, until Somali forces were within 200 kilometres of Addis Ababa.

The Soviets, believing that they could not allow an ally to be vanquished, decided to intervene in force. A secret military pact was agreed between Addis Ababa and Moscow in terms of which the Soviets would provide $385 million worth of arms. In return the Ethiopians cut ties with the United States. The Soviet Union then established an air-bridge to Ethiopia that lasted for the next eight months. Over this period 225 Soviet transport aircraft ferried supplies to Ethiopia, landing on average every twenty minutes. In the end Moscow's bill for supporting the Derg ran into many hundreds of millions of dollars. Estimates of the costs of Soviet support for the Derg down the years range from $1 billion to $4 billion.

A contingent of 11,600 Cuban troops and a further 6,000 military advisers were sent to bolster the Ethiopian war effort. Naturally the Cubans broke their ties with the Eritreans, who were seen as a threat to the Ethiopians. After the defeat of Somalia in March 1978, Soviet advisers began participating directly in the war against the Eritrean rebels, while advanced Soviet weapons were being used in the conflict. The Eritreans had learned that their links with Cuba would not survive, if it did not suit the interests of their erstwhile Soviet mentors.

Although the United States had lost Ethiopia as an ally, it chose not to support the Eritrean cause. This was, at least in part, because it distrusted the EPLF, which was by the late 1970s the major force inside Eritrea. The EPLF's Marxism was too overt for Washington's taste and the US instead continued to maintain what relations it could with the Ethiopian regime. Loans from the World Bank and IMF were approved and Washington provided vast quantities of aid through Addis Ababa when the terrible famine of 1984–85 struck. It was only in 1990, with the Derg on the ropes, that the US really intervened in the Horn in a major way. A conference, chaired by the Assistant Secretary of State for African Affairs, Herman Cohen, was held in London in May 1991. This paved the way for the Ethiopian leader Mengistu Haile Mariam going into exile in Zimbabwe, and for the TPLF, supported by the EPLF, to march into Addis Ababa. Demonstrators in the Ethiopian capital denounced what had transpired as 'Cohen's coup.' It was no such thing—the victory of the rebels was, by this point, inevitable: the US merely facilitated the transfer.

A more reliable—if less well resourced—source of support for the Eritreans came from Third World and Western socialists. A range of left-wing figures backed the Eritrean cause. These included the Tanzanian politician Abdulrahman Babu, the British historian Basil Davidson and the South African intellectual Ruth First. Lionel Cliffe was among a range of British scholars who supported Eritrean independence, travelling into EPLF controlled areas during the fight for independence. The British Labour Party recognised Eritrea's right to independence in 1981 and several prominent Labour politicians, including Glenys

Kinnock, visited 'the field'—as the areas of Eritrea held by EPLF rebels were known. British non-governmental organisations, in particular Oxfam and the church agencies, put resources behind the EPLF's relief organisation during the 1980s—especially during the terrible famine of 1984–85. The radical charity War on Want ran a consortium through which the aid was provided and was an outspoken advocate for the Eritreans.

The famine was an opportunity for the EPLF to show what it could do to meet the needs of the people. Grain, brought in by truck from Sudan, was distributed to the people, naturally winning their gratitude and support. Some of the aid was also siphoned off to purchase the arms and ammunition to meet the Ethiopian war-machine. There are also suggestions that the EPLF grew marijuana in substantial quantities in the areas under its control, using the foreign exchange the crop generated to purchase weaponry on the black market.

There follows a brief overview of Eritrean relations with various nations. They are all part of a web of ties that bind the Horn together, but have been characterised by complex manoeuvres over the years that have seen friends turn into enemies (sometimes overnight) only for the relationship to be cemented a few years later.

Sudan

It is probably accurate to say that no country was as important to Eritrean independence as Sudan. At the same time, the relationship between the Sudanese and the liberation movements was both complex and difficult. Support could turn to a clamp-down, and then be reversed, as the Sudanese authorities used the Eritreans in their frequent foreign policy manoeuvres. The Eritreans learnt to be acutely aware of the most minute changes in Sudanese policy and to keep in close personal touch with senior officials and politicians.

FOREIGN FRIENDS

The turmoil and repression of the 1960s saw tens of thousands of Eritrean refugees fleeing to neighbouring Sudan, to escape the harassment of the Ethiopian authorities. This only intensified once the armed struggle was launched. The Sudanese government was under pressure from Ethiopia to curb the activities of the ELF. When they failed to persuade Khartoum, the authorities in Addis Ababa began supporting southern Sudanese rebel movements, including the Anya Nya liberation front. A pattern was established: when Ethiopia wished to put pressure on the Sudanese they supported Sudanese rebellions. The Sudanese did the same in reverse, by providing or withholding aid to the Eritreans. The degree of freedom of action for Eritrean organisations operating in Sudan became a barometer of the Sudanese relationship with Ethiopia.

A case in point took place in 1972. There was a distinct but temporary improvement in relations between the two countries following the signing of the Addis Ababa Agreement ending seventeen years of war between the southern Sudanese and Khartoum. The Sudanese government of President Nimeiri responded by deploying his army to seal the Sudanese-Eritrean border, making life distinctly difficult for the Eritrean rebels. But matters didn't end there. In 1973 a group of Sudanese opposition parties based in Ethiopia (the Umma Party, Democratic Unionist Party, Sudanese Communist Party and the Muslim Brotherhood) formed a single body: the National Front. Backed by the Libyans, the National Front was used by the Ethiopians as a means of exerting pressure on the Nimeiri government. President Nimeiri responded by lifting the restrictions he had imposed and increasing his support for Eritrean movements, as well as Ethiopian rebel groups.

In May 1976 the Ethiopian military regime (the Derg) sent a delegation to Khartoum in an attempt to improve relations between the two governments. The delegation promised they would end their support for the National Front in return for Sudanese mediation with the Eritrean liberation movements. On 15 May 1976 the Derg presented a formal Nine Point Programme to end the Eritrean fight for independence. The Eritreans rejected the plan, since it only offered regional autonomy. In July the National Front attempted to overthrow Nimeiri. The Sudanese president held Ethiopia responsible for the failed coup and made a public statement supporting Eritrea's right to independence. He went further, warning that Sudan would raise an army from among the Eritrean and Ethiopian refugees living on its territory to oust the Ethiopian government, whom he described as 'Communist puppets'. This fanciful scheme came to nothing and Sudan's resolve gradually crumbled. By 1980 Ethiopia's President Mengistu was visiting Khartoum and Nimeiri was in Addis Ababa. Support for Eritrean causes was, once again, reduced.

In 1985 Nimeiri was overthrown and his place taken by Sadiq al-Mahdi. Al-Mahdi won an election the following year, only to be ousted in a coup in June 1989 by the Sudanese army, working with the National Islamic Front. This brought Omar al-Bashir to power, a position he has held ever since. Relations between the newly installed Islamist government and the secular EPLF were tense.

From rebels to government

The Eritreans were also suspicious that the Sudanese government were supporting their rivals: the Eritrean Islamic Jihad, which had been formed by the merger of four smaller movements in November 1988. The Jihadis pursued an Islamist agenda, wishing to establish a state based on Sharia law. Support for the Eritrean Islamic Jihad continued after the EPLF took Asmara in 1991 and even after Eritrea's formal independence in 1993. Their ranks may have even been strengthened by the inclusion of veterans who had fought in Afghanistan. In December 1994 the newly formed Eritrean government broke off diplomatic relations with Khartoum, stating that 'the Islamic government of Sudan... is opposed to the peace, security and stability of the people of Eritrea'.

Eritrea, flexing its muscles, stepped up its support for Sudanese opposition groups. In December 1994 these organisations met in Asmara and formed the Sudanese Alliance Forces. The Eritrean authorities were working with a range of disparate organisations, including the Sudan People's Liberation Army (which went on to become the government of South Sudan in 2011), the Democratic Unionist Party, Umma Party and the Communists. In order to step up their pressure on the Sudanese, the Eritrean government authorised their take-over of the Sudanese embassy in Asmara. The rebels now had the status of a government in exile and Eritrea encouraged them to overthrow the Sudanese government. As President Isaias told the *Economist* in October 1995: 'We are out to see that this [Sudanese] government is not there anymore. We are not trying to pressure them to talk to us, or to behave in a more constructive way. We will give weapons to anyone committed to overthrowing them.' Together with Uganda and Ethiopia (who were also keen to oust Omar al Bashir and were backed by the US) the Eritrean government moved against the Sudanese. This alliance gave their support to the southern rebels of the Sudan People's Liberation Movement.

They came close to achieving their goal. By spring of 1997 the Khartoum government had lost control of most of the 2,000 km of its eastern borders. The Sudanese army had also suffered serious setbacks in the south, losing the town of Kurmuk in Blue Nile province. The Sudanese rebels had considerable military support from Ethiopia. Addis Ababa had its own objectives here: to destroy the bases of two armed movements who had been operating from Sudan (the Oromo and Beni Shangul). The Sudanese government was looking distinctly vulnerable and might have fallen, had it not been for the outbreak of hostilities between Eritrea and Ethiopia in 1998.

When the war commenced, Ethiopia moved rapidly to mend fences with President al-Bashir. Eritrea did not, with predictable results. In March 1999 the Sudanese government allowed the Alliance of Eritrean National Forces, comprising ten opposition groups, to declare their intention of overthrowing President Isaias. This prompted an about-turn in Asmara, which launched a charm offensive against Khartoum. This was led by Hamad bin Khalifa Al-Thani, the emir of Qatar and a staunch ally of President Isaias. The emir brokered a rapprochement between Sudan and Eritrea, which led to the signing of a memorandum of understanding on 10 November 1998. In May 1999 the two presidents met in Doha to restore diplomatic relations and promised to refrain from 'hosting or organising regional or international conferences that aim to adopt tasks posing a threat to security and stability of neighbouring countries.' In due course the Sudanese rebel movements were asked to leave Eritrea. Sudan and Eritrea—previously at daggers drawn—were once again on good terms. In April 2002 the two countries exchanged ambassadors and, equally predictably, the Sudanese opposition was asked to leave the Sudanese embassy.

The rapprochement proved short-lived. By October 2002 Ethiopia, Yemen and Sudan had formed what was called the Sanaa Forum and Sudan was accusing Eritrea of sending its troops to fight in eastern Sudan. This was followed in 2004 by further accusations that Eritrean planes had transported weapons and ammunition to Darfur rebels in western Sudan. Eritrea was labelled a 'destablilising factor' in the region.

In January 2005 the politics of the region was shaken up once more. This time the catalyst was the peace agreement signed between the Sudanese government and the southern rebels of the Sudan People's Liberation Movement to be followed by the birth of South Sudan. With the SPLM having ended their conflict with Khartoum the Eritrean-backed alliance opposing the Sudanese government was severely weakened. By October 2005 an Eritrean delegation was once more in Khartoum and the laborious process of mending fences began again. This was finally sealed in June 2006, when Presidents Isaias and al-Bashir met in Khartoum. The formula they agreed to was a familiar one: Sudanese rebels would be restricted by the Eritreans, and vice-versa. Two years later President al-Bashir was in Asmara, visiting his opposite number. At least for the moment ties between these two neighbours had been restored.

Sudan unofficial

Given the incessant disruption of relations between the governments and their repeated support for each other's rebel movements, why is Sudan included in a chapter entitled 'Foreign Friends'? The answer is that despite the ups and downs of official policy, relations between the two nations are—on the whole—good. Some 125,000 Eritreans live in Sudan; many having done so for the last forty years. Sometimes Sudanese officials make their lives difficult and unpleasant, but for the most part they manage to get by. These exiles see life in Sudan as preferable to going home, something that has been offered them on several occasions.

In the second half of the 1950s the Eritrean Liberation Movement (the precursor to other Eritrean movements) opened an office in Sudan. During Eritrea's thirty years' war of independence (1961–1991) Sudan provided a relatively secure rear base from which to operate. Occasionally Ethiopian troops marauded across the border, but generally the ELF and the EPLF were able to operate from Sudanese soil. When I travelled into Eritrea in the 1980s I went via Port Sudan. The EPLF maintained a comfortable guest house in the city, which must have been well-known to the Sudanese police and security personnel. When it came to travelling into the liberated areas of Eritrea, trucks would simply drive across the remote semi-desert of eastern Sudan, picking up supplies at the ancient port of Suakin. Everything from fuel to tyres and spares was kept in a giant compound owned and operated by the Eritreans. From there it was on and across the border into Eritrea itself. These movements were regularised and authorised by senior Sudanese officials.

Thirty years later, little has changed. As the UN Monitors reported in 2014, 'a shared border, common kinship, and a long history of political involvement in the Sudan all gave the Government of Eritrea a distinct advantage in the region. The two countries share a 660 km-long undemarcated border where citizens and goods can move freely without visas and with minimal restrictions.'

Eritrea's long relationship with the peoples of eastern Sudan has paid dividends. The Eritrean sponsorship of the peace deal signed in 2006 between the Sudanese authorities and the groups fighting in the area cemented this accord. The UN Monitors report that a 'number of regional and national Sudanese officials... act as agents of Asmara. Governor Mohamed Taher Aila was consistently identified for his close personal relationship with President Afwerki.' General Manjus, the Eritrean officer responsible for security along the country's western border, is said to have subcontracted border patrolling to paramilitaries from the Rashaida ethnic group, which lives on both sides of the frontier.

This close relationship with eastern Sudan has allowed the Eritrean government to use Sudan as a major smuggling route for its weapons needs—by-passing the UN's sanctions. Small arms, trucks and ammunition have been imported into Eritrea via the town of Kassala. The UN says it has photographic evidence of these transfers. Forged bills of lading were allegedly provided, signed by Omar al-Naqi, Brigadier General of the Sudanese

Armed Forces and Director of General Security in Kassala. These allegations form part of the points raised with the Eritrean government by the UN Monitors. The reply was a routine denial.

The Eritrean relationship with Sudan does not end there. The UN reports provide evidence that Eritrean intelligence runs well-organised operations in both Khartoum and Juba. They control the smuggling operations, keeping tabs on the Sudanese and South Sudanese governments and monitoring the role of the large Eritrean diaspora in both countries. There are reports that the Eritrean ruling party run a number of businesses in Juba and in the Ugandan capital, Kampala. Some of these are commercial ventures for the benefit of senior Eritrean military and party officials. Using local businessmen as silent partners they own a range of firms, providing everything from restaurants to water and food distribution. It is through this network that the Eritrean government is reported to have provided support to Somali warlords and funds to various Somali groups.

Arabian friends

It is hard to assess just how important the Arab states across the Red Sea are to Eritrea, which has been intimately involved in the affairs of the states of the Arabian peninsula. Occasionally—particularly when Asmara's relations with Iran have been good—relations with the Arab world have gone into reverse. But this is not the norm. Most of these ties have been covert and private and therefore difficult to track. However, the work of the UN Monitors has proved extremely helpful in making sense of these activities. They provide a glimpse into the way in which personal ties (some of which can be traced back to the long war of independence) still play a major role in Eritrea's affairs. Trusted Eritreans use their influence in any way they can to enhance the interests of the party and the regime. There are no real boundar-

ıte relations, inter-personal connections and ques-
ːy.

̗raphs from the UN Monitor's 2011 report are quoted at length, since they give a flavour of what has been taking place:

> Dubai is a major hub for PFDJ [Eritrea's ruling party] offshore financial networks, serving as a conduit for much of the revenue—in the form of taxes, remittances and contributions—gathered by the Eritrean diaspora in North America, Europe and the Middle East. These funds can in turn be directed to a range of purposes, including Eritrean covert operations. This case study examines one potential route of PFDJ funds: from the United States, through Dubai and Nairobi, into the hands of armed opposition groups in Somalia and the Horn of Africa.

> Oakland, California, and the Washington, DC, area host some of the largest Eritrean communities in the United States, and therefore provide major sources of funding for PFDJ... some of this cash is deposited in Eritrean embassy bank accounts, but much of it is moved through increasingly opaque financial networks, employing money transfer companies and individual couriers. According to Eritrean sources, Tesfay (or Adey) Mariam is suspected of being one such financial facilitator. While working as a taxi driver in Arlington, Virginia, Tesfay Mariam—an Eritrean citizen with dual United States nationality—has organized the transfer of hundreds of thousands of dollars to Eritrean individuals and PFDJ-linked businesses in Dubai. Law enforcement agents have confirmed that a taxi driver resident in Virginia is involved in the transfer of illicit funds to Dubai, but did not provide the name of the individual.

> According to former Eritrean consular staff and Eritrean businessmen in Dubai, the Eritrean consulate in Dubai, and specifically the Commercial Attaché Mehari Woldeselassie, also play a central role in these arrangements. The consulate banks incoming revenues at an account with HSBC, a preferred bank of the Eritrean Government and PFDJ because of its global reach. In addition to supervising the operations of this account, Mr. Woldeselassie also manages procurement on

behalf of the Red Sea Corporation and coordinates commercial activities through some of the front companies mentioned above.

Senior Eritrean military figures travel regularly to Dubai, where they coordinate their financial transactions through the Dubai consulate. For example, General Teklai Habteselassie travelled to Dubai en route to Ukraine, in December 2009, in what a senior official of the Government of Eritrea has acknowledged was intended to be a military procurement mission General Te'ame Abraha and Colonel Tewelde Habte Negash regularly visit Dubai.

And Tesfalidet Habtesellasie, the most senior official in the President's office, travels frequently to China and Eastern Europe from Dubai. From Dubai, at least some of the hard currency stream is directed towards Nairobi, where the Eritrean embassy receives transfers into accounts under its control. Sources with access to financial transactions at the embassy have informed the Group that the embassy has used dollar-denominated accounts at Standard Chartered Bank and Barclays Bank in Nairobi to receive dollar deposits from abroad.

It is this nexus of political and personal relations that characterises Eritrea's ties with the Arab world. Frequently they can also spill over into issues of state security.

A player in the Yemeni civil war

Among the most controversial developments of recent years has been the Eritrean government's decision to enter the Yemeni civil war. Since 2004 the Houthis—tribesmen from northern Yemen, who follow the Shia branch of Islam—have been fighting the Yemeni government. For the Saudis and other Sunni governments in the Arabian peninsula this Shia uprising is seen as a major threat. In 2014–2015 the Houthis captured the Yemeni capital Sana'a, leading to the fall of the Saudi-backed government of Abd Rabbuh Mansur Hadi. This was interpreted as a victory for the Iranians, the arch-enemies of the Saudis, and the major

Shia power in the region. The Saudi government accused Iran of being the real force behind the Houthi revolt.

Unwilling to accept their loss of authority, the Saudis and their allies in the United Arab Emirates are reported to have turned to President Isaias. A number of sources, including the UN Monitors, describe how this took place. The UAE authorities are said to have first approached Djibouti, looking for rear bases from which to fight the Houthi; but Djibouti turned them down. The snub was wounding and on 4 May 2015 Djibouti and the UAE broke diplomatic relations. The Saudis, perhaps fearing this outcome, had already turned to Eritrea.

The *Indian Ocean Newsletter* reported that in April 2015 two delegations from Saudi Arabia and the UAE visited Eritrea, requesting the use of Eritrean ports and those Hanish islands that are part of Eritrean territory. It will be recalled that Eritrea fought with Yemen over control of the Hanish Islands in 1995–96, finally allowing the issue to be resolved by international arbitration. In the process Eritrea lost most of the islands, but some close to the Eritrean coast are apparently still useful as bases. The Eritreans offered the visiting delegations the use of their ports and the islands for operations in Yemen. It provided President Isaias with an opportunity to break out of Eritrea's diplomatic isolation and a valuable source of development assistance, since the Gulf States undertook to modernise Asmara airport and build new infrastructure.

In this tactical thaw with Asmara, the UAE and Saudi Arabia have performed something of a U-turn. In the past they opposed President Isaias, who had allowed Iran to use Eritrea as a base from which to supply arms to the Houthis and to train their fighters. Relations between Eritrea and the Saudis were cemented during a two-day visit to the kingdom by President Isaias in April 2015. In return for the assistance Eritrea is reported to have received fuel and finance. President Isaias has made no secret of this relationship. In an interview on Eritrean national television in January 2016, the president suggested a willingness to become more actively engaged in the region. 'Without taking limit, scope and size into consideration, collaboration of the regional countries is key,' he said, referring to Eritrea's involvement in the Yemen coalition. 'We can say that the announcement of this Saudi-led anti-terrorism effort is a small part of a bigger plan.'

The UN Monitors also received evidence that some 400 Eritrean troops were fighting alongside the UAE forces in Yemen, on behalf of the Arab coalition. This is a very powerful allegation to make, and it is worth noting the sources it came from. These are listed as:

> Telephone call with a former high-ranking Eritrean official with active ties to the Eritrean military, 22 August 2015; interview with an Eritrean political analyst with high-level contacts in the Middle East and Africa, 18 August 2015. This was substantiated by information received by a credible development source in direct contact with Eritrean officials and shared with the Monitoring Group on a highly confidential basis.

The allegations were given credibility by a report by Stratfor, a Texas based group of security analysts. In October 2015 they reported receiving satellite images of three landing craft belonging to the UAE docking in the Eritrean port of Assab on 16 September. *Jane's Defence Weekly* reported in April 2016 that the UAE appears to be 'constructing a new port next to Assab International Airport in Eritrea, which could become its first permanent military base in a foreign country.' The magazine says that satellite imagery shows rapid progress has been made since work began sometime after September 2015. A section of the coastline is being excavated, with a pier or breakwater being constructed, which already extends 700 metres from the original coastline. None of this is proof of what role President Isaias is playing in Yemen, but given the secretive nature of the Eritrean state, it is probably as good as it gets.

Voice of America—the US government's external broad-caster—examined these claims. They interviewed Michael Woldemariam, an assistant professor of international relations and political science at Boston University: 'There's a lot we don't know about what this cooperation looks like, what the arrangements look like,' Professor Woldemariam said. 'But from what I can tell, the main element of this cooperation is the use of Eritrea, particularly the port of Assab, as sort of a basic logistical hub from which states like Saudi Arabia and UAE are able to launch their operations into Yemen.'

Professor Woldemariam added that he believed fighter jets were also using Assab airport to attack Yemeni targets. But he said that he had not seen proof of Eritrean soldiers actually fighting with UAE units fighting in Yemen.

Eritreans living in Yemen confirm the presence of Eritrean forces on the ground. How many of them are involved in the conflict is not clear, but there seems to be little doubt that they have become participants in the fighting. As if the story was not complex enough, the UN Monitors also said they had seen a pattern of Eritrean support for the Houthi rebels over a number of years. This is a murky story indeed.

The European Union

Since independence, relations between Asmara and Washington have been difficult, with few moments of real warmth. The US has for many years seen Ethiopia as the more important player in the Horn of Africa. As a result, as noted above, Washington failed to put real pressure on Addis Ababa over the question of the border demarcation and this badly soured its relationship with Asmara. Relations between Asmara and Brussels have been more complex, with attempts on the part of the Europeans to have a more constructive dialogue, but with only limited success.

The European's response to Eritrea developed over many years. It should not be forgotten that Europe supported the Eritrean people well before the de-facto independence of the country in 1991, especially during the 1984–85 famine, when European countries were major donors. Cross-border operations fed hundreds of thousands of people who would otherwise have starved.

Europe attempted to build a strong relationship with the Eritrean government once it had achieved independence. Despite Eritrea's repression and its record of human rights abuses the EU has tried to maintain its ties with the regime. This has been difficult to achieve. The problem was perhaps most starkly highlighted during the 2001 clampdown on all forms of opposition, with the imprisonment of senior politicians, journalists and editors. Among those who were arrested then is Dawit Isaak, a Swedish-Eritrean journalist who has been held in detention ever since. His status as a Swede meant the EU has repeatedly called for his release and EU representatives have repeatedly taken up his case: all to no avail.

When the arrests took place the Italian ambassador to Eritrea, Antonio Bandini, presented a letter of protest to the authorities. He was promptly expelled from the country. Other European ambassadors were withdrawn in protest. The EU presidency said relations between the EU and Eritrea had been 'seriously undermined' by the government's action. At first the Europeans demanded that Eritrea improve its human rights before normal relations were resumed. President Isaias did nothing of the sort, assuming that he could contain and diffuse the EU's anger. He was proved right: in the end it was the Europeans who buckled. They needed to find partners in the Horn of Africa with whom they could work. Eritrea was too strategically important and too troublesome to be ignored. European politicians, officials and diplomats were under pressure to find solutions. By contrast, President Isaias was answerable to no one and therefore immune to EU pressure or persuasion.

An internal EU document dated October 2008 explained just how poorly the EU had responded to the situation. The report said that it had been decided at the time that European ambassadors would be: 'conditioning their return on the willingness of President Isaias to engage on human rights dialogue. This request was never satisfied, but EU Ambassadors nevertheless returned to Eritrea, in a non-coordinated way.' The Europeans had sent an important message to Asmara; one that the regime was quick to grasp. All they had to do was wait and the EU would come cap in hand; and so it proved.

In May 2007 President Isaias was invited to visit Brussels and was 'warmly welcomed' by the Development Commissioner, Louis Michel, despite the fact that Dawit Isaak and the others remained in prison. In the light of the talks at the European Commission the EU altered its stance towards Eritrea, as the internal report made clear:

> In June 2007 the European Commission changed its strategy and initiated a process of political re-engagement with Eritrea. The main reason for Commissioner Louis Michel's change of approach was his determination to ignite a positive regional agenda for the Horn of Africa, where Eritrea has a major role to play in view of its presence in the conflicts in Sudan and Somalia.

The document concluded that for this 'political re-engagement' to work both sides would be required to show that they were serious about it. Concrete evidence was required:

> Both sides need political dialogue to bring some results: the European Commission needs a visible sign of cooperation from Eritrea in order to continue to justify its soft diplomacy, while the increasingly isolated Eritrean regime might need to keep a credible interlocutor and a generous donor. The liberation of Dawit Isaak based on humanitarian grounds could be such a sign but, although welcome, it would only be a drop in the ocean.

Although no 'visible sign' emerged and there was no real progress, fresh aid was promised and then provided to Eritrea. Instead of making improvements to human rights, the Eritrean government refused to accommodate the EU's concerns in any way. Despite this the Europeans pressed ahead with their 'renewed engagement' strategy. Brussels had learnt nothing from the mistakes made following the withdrawal of its ambassadors. Asmara, on the other hand, had realised that if it remained obdurate European politicians and civil servants would, in time, give in to its demands. President Isaias was setting the agenda.

On 2 September 2009 the EU and Eritrea signed a 'Country Strategy for 2009–2013'. This acknowledged the impact of Eritrea's 2001 crackdown on dissent, albeit in diplomatic language. 'From 2001 to 2003, there was a slowdown in EU-Eritrea development cooperation, and the Political Dialogue process witnessed the emergence of substantially divergent views on developments in Eritrea and the Region.' The report talked about 'limited' political dialogue, but said that regular meetings were planned.

A mission by the Development Committee of the European Parliament in late 2008 painted a more gloomy, albeit more accurate, picture. The fact-finding mission by a delegation from the Committee found that: 'Since the interruption of the democratisation process in 2001, EC cooperation with Eritrea has been confronted with major political and technical difficulties. Cooperation was frozen for several years in reaction to the expulsion of the Italian Ambassador, which led to a certain backlog with the 9th EDF funds.' At the same time the delegation maintained that the situation had improved sufficiently in recent years and funds had begun to flow once more.

Apparently hopeful that progress could be made, the Development Commissioner, Louis Michel, opened fresh talks with Eritrea. By August 2009 he was sufficiently encouraged to visit Asmara, after receiving assurances from an Eritrean diplomat that Dawit Isaak would be released into his care. Having booked a ticket for Dawit to return with him to Europe, Louis Michel left for Asmara. But once he met President Isaias it became immediately apparent that he had no intention of allowing Dawit to go free. Indeed, Mr Michel was not even permitted to visit the prisoner, and had to return home without him, Dawit's unused ticket in his pocket.

These setbacks did not persuade the EU to abandon its policy of attempting to placate Eritrea. In October 2009, despite the fiasco of the Michel visit, European foreign ministries were prepared to take a considerably softer line towards Eritrea than their American counterparts. A US diplomatic cable, released via Wikileaks, reported how one European representative after another called for restraint, while opposing extending sanctions against the Afwerki regime:

> Italy described Eritrea as governed by a 'brutal dictator,' and noted that Italy had not gotten results from its efforts at engagement. He cautioned, however, against 'creating another Afghanistan' by applying Eritrea-focused sanctions. The Italian representative questioned whether the sanctions should be focused on spoilers in general and include others beyond Eritrea. The French said that while engagement was 'useless,' France would continue on this track as there was no other option.

Speaking at the same day-long meeting the British official Jonathan Allen explained his government's position: 'London has already made clear to Asmara that the UK was aware Eritrea was supporting anti-Western groups that threatened British security.' In reply the American senior representative, the Deputy Assistant Secretary for African Affairs, Karl Wycoff pointed out what was described as: 'the inconsistency between the private acknowledgement that Asmara was not only playing a spoiler role with regard to Somalia but also supporting violent, anti-West elements and the provision by some countries [of] assistance packages to Asmara. He also noted that strong actions, including sanctions, were needed to have a chance of changing Isaias's behaviour.' Despite the American concerns the EU pressed ahead with its strategy: a strategy in which it had little faith and which its representatives described as 'useless'.

The situation was reviewed in 2011 once more, when the EU drew up a 'Strategic Framework for the Horn of Africa.' This laid out Europe's relationship with the region as a whole: 'The EU is heavily engaged in the region, with involvement focused around five main areas: the development partnership, the political dialogue, the response to crises, the management of crises and the trade relationship.'

The document then elaborates on how this would be achieved. Once again human rights was an integral part of the strategy:

The development of democratic processes and institutions that contribute to human security and empowerment will be supported through:

- promoting respect for constitutional norms, the rule of law, human rights, and gender equality through cooperation and dialogue with Horn partners;
- support to security sector reform and the establishment of civilian oversight bodies for accountable security institutions in the Horn countries;
- implementing the EU human rights policy in the region

In line with these policies it was decided to provide Eritrea with aid worth €122 million between 2009 and 2013.

Since the Strategic Framework document was drawn up the situation inside Eritrea has shown no sign of improvement. Although the EU continued to raise the human rights situation there has been no progress on the release of political prisoners, the implementation of the Constitution or on freedom of expression. The country remains a one-party state, locked into permanent repression. Human rights violations continue to drive four to five thousand Eritreans across its borders every month. Many arrive on European shores. In the first ten months of

2014, for example, the number of asylum seekers arriving in Europe nearly tripled, according to the UN Refugee Agency. In 2015 a total of 38,791 people crossed the central Mediterranean, arriving mostly in Italy, according to FRONTEX—the EU agency monitoring the situation. Eritrea remained one of the top ten countries from which illegal arrivals came.

The refugee question has become a toxic issue in Europe. Politicians are under pressure to end illegal migration from all sources. Borders have been closed, fences erected and passport controls reinstated. While the Eritrean case is very different from that of Iraqi or Syrian refugees, they have been caught up in the rising tide of opposition to foreigners of all kinds. A number of European states have been attempting to respond to this, and have—once again—attempted a 'new engagement' with Asmara. In 2014 the Danish government sent officials to Eritrea to investigate the situation. They then wrote a report that was published by the Danish Immigration Service report. This concluded: that: 'the human rights situation in Eritrea may not be as bad as rumoured.'

The Danish report was not well received by scholars and human rights activists. It was inaccurate and misquoted the key academic source that it relied on. Professor Gaim Kibreab, whose work featured heavily in the Danish report, said he felt 'betrayed' by the way in which it was used. 'I was shocked and very surprised. They quote me out of context. They include me in a context with their anonymous sources in order to strengthen their viewpoints. They have completely ignored facts and just hand-plucked certain information.' Two of the three Danish authors resigned in disagreement with the report's conclusions and the Danish Immigration Service decided not to use it. Despite this, the report continued to have considerable currency. It was picked up by a number of European nations, including the UK.

The British sent their own officials to Asmara and they returned with similar conclusions. In March 2015 the UK's position on the country suddenly changed. The Home Office published updated country guidance suggesting a marked improvement in Eritrea's human rights situation. This was interpreted by British bureaucrats as a sign that they should treat Eritrean requests for asylum less sympathetically. The acceptance rate for Eritrean refugees promptly plummeted from 84 per cent in 2014 to 44 per cent in 2015. When these cases were taken to the courts the British judiciary was not persuaded that Eritrean human rights had really improved. Data obtained under the Freedom of Information Act shows that from March 2015 (when the changes were introduced) to September 2015, 1,006 out of 1,179 Eritreans rejected by the Home Office decided to appeal. Of the 118 cases in progress under the same time period, 106 were allowed. That is an appeal success rate of 92 per cent, which is considerably above the average for appeals.

The idea that Eritrea was 'improving' had gained credibility over the last few years. It appeared only a matter of time before there would be yet another attempt to launch a 'fresh engagement' with the Eritrean government. This was reflected in a publication by the Royal Institute of International Affairs—Chatham House. Jason Mosely wrote:

> The creation of the position of the EU Special Representative (EUSR) for the Horn of Africa in 2012 offers the possibility of a new kind of engagement between the EU and both Eritrea and Ethiopia. In terms of engagement with Eritrea, in particular, the EU is hampered on two fronts. First, as a guarantor of the Algiers Agreement, its influence in Eritrea has suffered from its perceived failure to enforce compliance by Ethiopia. Second, the EU also has a diplomatic stance rooted in a human-rights based approach to foreign policy, although it is not the only actor in the region in this regard. Neither of these factors leaves it well placed to act as an 'honest broker' from Asmara's perspective.

> However, the EUSR, Alex Rondos, has managed to cultivate a functional relationship with Eritrea. With the goal of improving overall

regional stability in mind, and thus consistent with his mandate, it is possible that his office could play an important role in improving relations between Eritrea and the EU and its member states.

The somewhat dismissive reference to human rights suggested that rights are regarded as an inconvenient adjunct to foreign policy, an encumbrance that might be disposed of. It accurately reflected the mood within the EU Council of Ministers.

In 2014 Italy's Deputy Minister of Foreign Affairs, Lapo Pistelli, made an official visit to Asmara. He was fulsome in his praise for his hosts, saying that he found them 'well informed and keen to engage.' The enthusiasm with which he greeted this 'new beginning' was reflected in the official communiqué from the Italian government. 'It's time for a new start,' Pistelli declared during his visit to Asmara. 'I am here today to bear witness to our determination to revitalise our bilateral relations and try to foster Eritrea's full reinstatement as a responsible actor and key member of the international community in the stabilisation of this region.' It was almost as if the setbacks of the past had never taken place.

The Khartoum process

Since then the EU has attempted to deal with Eritrea as part of a wider African initiative to try to end the exodus across the Mediterranean. In October 2014 senior European officials met with their African opposite numbers in Khartoum, including Eritrea. During this gathering Eritrea's Minister of Foreign Affairs, Osman Saleh, told the gathering that:

> Eritrea values its partnership with the European Union and is determined to work with the EU and all European countries to tackle irregular migration and human trafficking and to address their root causes. *We call for an urgent review of European migration policies towards Eritreans*, as they are, to say the least, based on incorrect information,

something that is being increasingly acknowledged [emphasis in the original].

The Khartoum meeting came up with a series of rather vaguely phrased suggestions aimed at reducing smuggling and human trafficking. This became known as the 'Khartoum Process' and was endorsed by the EU in December 2014.

In November 2015 a much higher profile meeting was held in the Maltese capital, Valetta. The Valetta summit, which again included Eritrea, brought together African leaders and their European counterparts. Designed to deal with the refugee crisis the political communiqué that was released contained little that was controversial. It concluded that: 'We recognise the high degree of interdependence between Africa and Europe as we face common challenges that have an impact on migration: promoting democracy, human rights, eradicating poverty, supporting socio-economic development, including rural development, mitigating and adapting to the effects of climate change.'

Buried in the summit's Action Plan that accompanied the communiqué were a series of recommendations. These included a recognition that African states bear the greatest burden of refugees, only a minority of whom actually make the journey to Europe. There was also an understanding that the African refugee camps in which so many languish needed to be upgraded. Security in the camps had to be improved, and education and entertainment should be provided, so that young men and women were not simply left to rot. There were even suggestions that some—a tiny, educated minority—might be allowed to travel via legal routes to European destinations.

Paragraph 4 of the document contained more worrying suggestions. There were details of how European institutions would co-operate with their African partners to fight 'irregular migration, migrant smuggling and trafficking in human beings'. This aim was laudable enough, until one considered them through the eyes of a refugee struggling to get past Eritrea's border force, with strict instructions to shoot to kill. Europe was offering training to African 'law enforcement and judicial authorities' in new methods of investigation and 'assisting in setting up specialised anti-trafficking and smuggling police units.' The European police forces of Europol and the EU's border force (FRONTEX) would in future assist African security police in countering the 'production of forged and fraudulent documents.'

Promises of technical support and intelligence sharing were followed by an offer of aid. On 11 December 2015 the EU announced that it intended to provide €200 million worth of aid for Eritrea. Most was allocated to the energy sector and what was described as strengthening the country's ability to 'better manage public finances.' Announcing the programme, EU Commissioner for International Co-operation and Development, Neven Mimica, said:

> The EU provides development aid where it is most needed to reduce poverty and support people. In Eritrea, we have agreed to promote activities with concrete results for the population, such as the creation of job opportunities and the improvement of living conditions. At the same time, we are insisting on the full respect of human rights as part of our ongoing political dialogue with Eritrea.

The idea that Eritrea would accept the EU's conditions on human rights suggests the Europeans have learnt very little from its past experiences. There is no evidence that the Eritrean government has ever been willing to accept aid conditionality of any kind. This is likely to be a dialogue of the deaf, with President Isaias ignoring European demands, secure in the knowledge that they have little option but to deal with Eritrea on his terms.

In the meantime a consensus developed among European officials that human rights organisations had exaggerated how serious the situation was in Eritrea. It looked as if it was only a matter of time before Eritreans claiming asylum across Europe would have their refugee claims rejected, and they were put on an aircraft home. This was strengthened by suggestions—from Eritrean diplomats and officials—that within a few months all National Service conscripts would only be required to serve eighteen months. This illusion soon fell apart.

In February 2016 the Reuters news agency carried a report, quoting EU diplomats. Speaking on conditions of anonymity they 'accused Eritrea of back-tracking on privately made commitments by some officials last year to fix national service at 18 months, a term stipulated four years after Eritrea's independence from Ethiopia in 1991.' President Isaias had done what he has done so often in the past. He had allowed (and possibly even encouraged) his officials to give assurances to gain a deal with an international partner, only to pull the rug from under the pledges they had given. This was followed by a two-week visit to Eritrea by Swiss and German diplomats, who toured Eritrea in March but were not allowed to see prison or military facilities. Accompanied by Eritrean officials, they gathered information that could 'help them better understand the situation in the country and verify asylum seekers' stories,' as the official Swiss press release put. But Mario Gattiker, the head of the Swiss State Secretariat for Migration, told the *Tages-Anzeiger* newspaper that although there had been 'indications' that Eritrea had reduced conscription to eighteen months, 'those hopes did not turn out to be true. Eritrea officially went back on its promise of shortening the required national military service. And the proof of improved human rights conditions is still missing,' Gattiker said.

What is extraordinary is just how easily the diplomatic community was taken in. The Reuters report quoted an unnamed Western diplomat as saying about the Eritreans: 'They are engaging more... You have to build their confidence. They don't move quickly.' Even the language is re-cycled. The only aspect that remains unchanging is President Isaias's intransigence.

Despite these setbacks European diplomats and civil servant have been under intense pressure to find some way of ending the African refugee exodus. They proceeded with the plans outlined in Malta, despite the risks these entailed. The civil servants were fully aware of what this involved. In May 2016 the German magazine, *Der Spiegel* and the television programme 'Report Mainz' uncovered details of the EU's plans, which involved a programme of co-operation with some of Africa's most notorious regimes.

The magazine reported that Germany was leading this work, but that the European Commission had warned that 'under no circumstances' should the public learn about what was being considered. A staff member working for Federica Mogherini, the EU High Representative for Foreign Affairs, said that Europe's reputation could be at stake if the details became public. Nor were they unaware of the dangers that co-operation with African security services might hold. Under the heading 'Risks and assumptions' the EU document states: 'Provision of equipment and trainings [sic] to sensitive national authorities (such as security services or border management) diverted for repressive aims; criticism by NGOs and civil society for engaging with repressive governments on migration (particularly in Eritrea and Sudan).'

The detailed proposals outlined a range of requirements for nine African states, from Uganda to Djibouti. The most controversial involve proposed deals with Sudan, Eritrea and Ethiopia. The Sudanese President Omar al Bashir was wanted for war crimes by the International Criminal Court; Eritrea was being investigated by the UN for crimes against humanity; Ethiopia has repressed its largest ethnic group, the Oromo people. Despite these gross violations of human rights the plans envisaged Sudan receiving a range of computers, scanners, cameras, cars and all the necessary training at seventeen border crossing points. Two 'reception centres' were proposed at Gadaref and Kassala, on Sudan's eastern border with Ethiopia and Eritrea.

The Eritreans were promised training for the judiciary and what was described as 'Assistance to develop or implement human trafficking regulations.' No doubt this would involve working with Eritrea's notoriously corrupt border force. The EU itself admitted that its planned partner states were riddled with corruption—often involving the officials who would have to implement these policy recommendations:

> Smuggling and trafficking networks in the region are highly organised and sophisticated, often with the complicity of officials... Corruption is reported to be widespread in almost every beneficiary country, facilitating illegal migration and trafficking through the complicity of ticket bureaux, check-in-desks, immigration officials, border patrols, etc.

Despite these identified risks the proposals have been taken forward. An EU spokesman denied that these plans had not yet been implemented. But when pressed on whether the documents were forgeries, the spokesman made no reply.

* * *

From this brief review of Eritrea's foreign relations a number of trends are clear. Firstly, that a great deal is done covertly. Informal relationships have always been vitally important to Eritreans, who are clearly comfortable operating in this way. After all, there are just a few million Eritreans worldwide and working through personal relationships is not difficult. The most important foreign relations continued in this way even after the EPLF took Asmara in 1991 and achieved full statehood in 1993. President Isaias keeps a tight reign on the networks that he controls, both inside and outside the country.

Secondly, relations have frequently been ruptured when this suited the president, and just as rapidly repaired. This reflects the informal nature of his dealings, which he directly and personally controls. Often changes of policy are the result of little more than Isaias's whims. Eritrean diplomats have frequently complained that they are left powerless and required to sweep up the mess that he has landed the country in.

On the plus side is the third characteristic: that Eritrea has no qualms about changing sides and can react rapidly to crises. President Isaias had no compunction about changing sides in the Yemeni conflict. And this is by no means the only example. Eritrea, although frustrated by and suspicious of the United States' intentions following the 1998–2000 border war with Ethiopia was, nonetheless, willing to consider a different approach in 2002. In that year President Isaias appeared keen to offer the United States naval bases in the country. In November 2002 brigadier general John Costello of the US Navy's Central Command held talks with Sebhat Ephrem, Minister of Defence. Then, in December, President Isaias told the US Defence Secretary, Donald Rumsfeld, that his country could have access to Eritrea's military bases as part of its war against terror. Rumsfeld, on a four-nation tour of the Horn, did not say whether the US would take up the offer, but the gesture was nonetheless genuine.

Since independence relations with Ethiopia have moved from warm to cool, then to conflictual. Now they are frozen; yet it would not be difficult to imagine how they might alter once more. It seems highly unlikely that this will take place while President Isaias is in power. The Ethiopian government is essentially waiting until Isaias leaves the scene, one way or another. Some Ethiopians are still not reconciled to Eritrean independence, but they are a minority. Addis Ababa is presently concentrating on developing alternative routes to the sea, by supporting the construction of a new port being built by Djibouti at Tadjourah. If a new leader (or leadership) emerges in Eritrea there could well be a thawing of relations.

It is worth noting the difficulty of describing a state's foreign policy when so much is covert, personal and subject to such swift alteration. What remains is information about those parts of the iceberg that protrude above the waves. Apart from this, there are just ripples on the surface of Eritrea's complex and fraught foreign policies.

Finally, there is the difficulty that western states have had in coming to grips with a regime that is so unwilling to enter into a serious dialogue with them. President Isaias's intransigence has left both Washington and Brussels floundering about in an attempt to fashion a coherent policy towards Eritrea: a minor but strategically significant state, in a troubled region.

6

FROM FREEDOM TO DICTATORSHIP

How was it that Eritrea, which won independence in 1991, and became a respected, internationally recognised nation in 1993, has sunk so far in just over two decades? Once hailed as a beacon of hope for the Horn of Africa and a possible 'Singapore' of the region, it is now mired in poverty, repression and bitter recriminations with almost all its neighbours.

The answer can be traced, in good measure, to the personality and policies of one man: Isaias Afwerki. At seventy he has been both the towering figure who led his people to independence and the dictator who now holds them in servitude. Without understanding something about him there is little chance of grasping the current situation. Eritrean culture recognises the heroic leader. As a Tigrinya proverb puts it: 'Whoever reigns is my King; that which rises (from the East) is my Sun.' Yet, whatever his weaknesses, Isaias has done little to encourage a cult of personality. Asmara is not a city littered by his portrait or dominated by giant North Korean statues of the 'great leader' of the kind that can be found in other African capitals. But the president has made such an indelible imprint on his nation that it is simply impossible to understand Eritrea without grasping something about its president.

The enigma of Isaias

Isaias was born on 2 February 1946 in the Aba Shi'aul district of Asmara—a working class suburb of the city. His father was an official with the state tobacco monopoly, while his grandmother was a migrant from Tigray. His paternal grandfather was a soldier who served with Ras Alula, the Tigrayan prince who was one of the greatest Ethiopian generals of the nineteenth century. Isaias father's village was Tselot, close to the outskirts of Asmara. Visitors who have been to the village in recent years report that it is still unmodernised: donkeys roam the streets, with no running water or sewerage. The simple houses enjoy dramatic views down the escarpment to the plain below.

Isaias spent most of his youth in Asmara. He went to the Prince Makonnen Secondary School. Woldeyesus Ammar, a leading member of the ELF, quotes his schoolmates as saying that he was known for making derogatory remarks about Muslims. The school was one of only two publicly funded schools that was attended by many of Eritrea's future leaders. Like them Isaias became involved in secret nationalist politics even before leaving to study engineering at the Haile Selassie University in Addis Ababa in 1965. He—along with fellow Eritrean students, Mussie Tesfamikael and Woldeyesus Ammar—maintained his interest in Eritrean politics. Just how much Isaias was really engaged in politics is questionable: some of his fellow ELF members at the university recall him missing meetings of the party cell.

Isaias's studies did not progress well. He failed his June 1966 exams and was forced to repeat his first year. Without funding for food or lodging from the university it was not a tempting prospect. Isaias told his comrades that he had decided to leave, to join the ELF in the field. On 17 October of that year Mussie, Woldeyesus and several others of his comrades spent the night with him in the Merkato bus station in Addis Ababa, seeing him off for Asmara. From the Eritrean capital Isaias travelled to Kassala in eastern Sudan. There he was joined by two others: Mussie (who was executed by Isaias in 1974) and Haile Wold'ensae, better known as 'Drue' (who went on to become Eritrea's foreign minister). The three men founded a clandestine organisation.

Haile, who had been with Isaias at university in Ethiopia, described in an interview with Dan Connell how his friend received him when he arrived at Kassala in late December 1966. 'I knocked on the door—in fact, Isaias was the one who opened the gate—and the first thing he told me was that I have to shut my mouth, that he's going to tell me a lot of things.' Haile was told to register his presence but to make no further comment.

'I was shocked,' Haile recalls. 'What happened to this guy? Why is he so afraid?' It turned out that the ELF, which had begun in the western lowlands among Muslim Eritreans had few highland Christians in its ranks. Men like Isaias and Haile had assumed it was an exemplary revolutionary organisation. The movement did not live up to their expectations. Its leadership was poor and sectarian. Isaias, who had already shown his suspicions of Muslims, believed it was hostile to its Christian recruits. This was a shock for these young idealists. 'This was a very dark moment for us,' said Haile. To confront it Isaias, Haile and Mussie decided they needed to form a clandestine, tight-knit cell. This form of organisation was banned by the ELF—'This was a very dangerous endeavour,' Haile told Connell. To seal their pact the three men took an oath, which they signed in their own blood. They carved an 'E' on their right arms—symbolising their determination to live or die for Eritrea.

It is perhaps worth pausing here, for what had taken place tells us a good deal about Isaias and the men he surrounded himself with, even at this early age. An idealistic nationalist he had shown himself little interested in academic life. Practical and down to earth, he had little patience with intellectual activity: what mattered was progress towards freeing his country from Ethiopian rule. Addis Ababa University was—at this time—a hub of left-wing student activism, and Isaias probably brought with him some of these views. But it was his reaction to what he found out about the ELF in Sudan that really marked him out. This tall, good looking young man, was determined not to give up the struggle. Far from becoming disgruntled and down heartened when the organisation failed to live up to his expectations, he organised: and organised subversively.

Taking a secret oath, signed in blood, to establish a clandestine party-within-a-party marked Isaias out as the kind of driven revolutionary with real leadership potential. Not for him the slow climb through the ranks, the doffing of his cap to the current party bosses. Isaias would use secretive structures and personal dedication to take him to the top. The Eritrean penchant for discretion suited Isaias down to the ground. A covert and manipulative management of his movement, and finally the affairs of the Eritrean state, became the hallmarks of his leadership style. Colleagues have been endlessly moved between positions to leave them uncertain of their status and dependent on his favour. As a journalist I had the opportunity to interview him—both during the EPLF's time as a guerrilla movement and after the capture of Asmara in 1991. It was an experience that left me feeling distinctly uneasy (even before the regime rounded up all independent journalists in 2001.) Isaias combined bombast with a poorly disguised contempt for the media. His idea of an interview has always consisted of a lengthy, but unrevealing, tirade.

FROM FREEDOM TO DICTATORSHIP

In 1967 Isaias, and four others (including the EPLF's future secretary general, Ramadan Mohammed Nur) left for China to further their political and military studies. This was at the start of the Cultural Revolution and China was a country in ferment. President Liu Shaoqi and other Communist leaders were removed from power. Beaten and imprisoned, Liu died in prison two years later. Factions of the Red Guard movement were battling for supremacy on the streets of Chinese cities that were only saved from anarchy in September 1967, when Mao had Lin send the army in to restore order. The young Eritreans must have looked on amazed—but for someone of Isaias's calibre there was much to grasp. Mao, an authoritarian leader, who had seen the need to turn his society upside down to strengthen its revolutionary zeal, was someone the young Eritrean could emulate.

Founding the EPLF

Isaias and Ramadan began making derogatory remarks about the ELF, and soon fell out with their Eritrean comrades, who threatened that this would be sorted out when they returned home. They were not deterred, making notes of how best to form a clandestine party. When the time came to leave China instead of making his way to Sudan, Isaias went to Saudi Arabia, attempting to cross into Eritrea by dhow. He was arrested and held for nearly six months before Osman Saleh Sabbe, a senior ELF leader, could negotiate his release.

By the time he returned in 1968 the ELF was in turmoil. The organisation had divided its forces into five divisions. Isaias was sent to be political commissar of the 5th division to his home region, Hamasien, which surrounds Asmara. The division was composed mostly of Christians. Isaias and others who shared his views were deeply opposed to the religious segregation of the movement. He joined a reform movement known as 'Eslah' in

Arabic. Its members were mainly composed of younger, more educated activists—including those who had been trained in Syria, Cuba and China. With the ELF beset by bitter in-fighting Isaias then joined one of its factions: the Popular Liberation Forces (PLF2) which decided to withdraw from the ELF. Isaias then led the group into an alliance with other breakaway factions to form the Eritrean Liberation Forces—People's Liberation Front. Osman Saleh Sabbe, who had rescued him from a Saudi prison, served as the movement's foreign representative in Cairo, supplying them with arms until their relationship ended in 1976.

Away from prying eyes, in the deserts of the Danakil in eastern Eritrea an even more important event was taking place. This was the formation of the Eritrean People's Revolutionary Party—often referred to simply as the 'People's Party'. Its secret membership led by Isaias and his closest associates, it was founded on 4 April 1971. As one of the founders, Mahmoud Sherifo, told Dan Connell: 'We met there and discussed the need to form a core among us before uniting the new forces, to campaign on the basis of nationalism and progressive ideas... to [get] rid of the prejudices and grudges of the past. We decided to work in a very secretive manner. Marxism would be our leading ideology...' This was precisely the way Isaias had worked ever since he had been a schoolboy. It was the culmination of the practices he had established with his closest confidants and signed in blood in Sudan.

Woldeyesus Ammar, writing from the perspective of the ELF, had a rather different take on these events. He accuses Isaias of having written to friends in the highlands as early as 1968, urging them to send as many Christians to join the fight as possible, to defend the 'dignity' of their people. When the break with the ELF came in November 1971, according to Woldeyesus, Isaias made it plain that he saw them as an oppressed group within the wider movement. Isaias is said to have declared in the group's founding document, *Nehnan Elamanan* ('We and our Goals'):

'What do you do when they chase you out of what you thought was a national cause? What do you do when they oppress you while fighting for freedom?' To address this oppression Isaias and his colleagues are said to have established their own organisation, which drew its support from the highland community, even if 'almost all or even all of us are Christians by birth, by culture and by history'. According to this narrative, it was a desire by Isaias to enhance the position of Christians within the liberation struggle, as opposed to any faults with the ELF, that led to the rupture with the party.

Yet even at this early stage in the formation of what became the EPLF Isaias did not have things all his own way. Before he could assert his supremacy over his movement he had to rebuff two internal challenges: from left and from right. Binding a close-knit group of supporters around him he saw off both of them. The left wing faction was led by his old friend, Mussie Tesfamikael, with whom Isaias has taken his blood-oath. The internal debate that surrounded this split was important. Mussie, informed by the left-wing Marxist ideology then prevalent among revolutionary movements in the developing world, called for more radical policies. He also criticised the lack of democratic decision-making within the new organisation. Mussie and his supporters met in secret late at night—leading to their nickname: *menqa*—the bats. They underestimated Isaias. He denounced his critics in a publication entitled: 'The destructive movement of 1973'. Isaias mobilised his supporters, established a committee to try them and rounded up the *menqa*. The principle of 'innocent until proven guilty' was reversed and became 'guilty until proven innocent.' As many as eleven may have been arrested and jailed—some of them for years. Mussie suffered an even harsher fate. Together with a colleague he was executed on 11 August 1974.

The *Yameen* (Arabic for 'right') movement proved easier to resist. This was purged by an internal security organisation known as 'the guardian of the revolution.' The 'guardian' routinely tortured anyone they suspected of disloyalty—including new recruits, just in case they turned out to be infiltrators. Professor Gaim Kibreab quotes Michael Ghaber, a prominent ELF dissident and historian who was active in the 1960s, as pointing out how severe the problems of security were for the early Eritrean movements, which were subjected to intense scrutiny by the Ethiopians. 'In the early phases of the resistance, trust was a luxury that we could not afford. It was safer to be suspicious.' The problem was that this became entrenched in the movements. Professor Gaim concludes:

A slight deviation, on matters of procedure let alone substance, was interpreted as a betrayal of the organisation and its goals. The practice that began in the early 1960s became entrenched as norms throughout the 30 years of war, even in the liberated areas where there was no imminent threat from the enemy. From the early 1970s onwards as the independence movement splintered, an ominous element was added to the cocktail of fear and suspicion as betrayal could come from rival factions as well as from agents of the Ethiopian state.

Dr Bereket Habte Selassie, the widely respected Chairman of the Constitutional Commission after independence, witnessed this in the spring of 1976 when he was travelling through areas inside Eritrea under the movement's control. 'I heard about widespread practice of torture under Solomon [Woldemariam's] watch. I dismissed the rumours as enemy propaganda, or factional spite,' he later recalled. But one day, while going to the toilet, he heard cries coming from the bush. There, to his horror, he found Solomon's deputy beating a man about the head. 'The victim, whose hands and feet were tied and who apparently knew me, called me by my name and begged to be rescued.' But Dr Bereket was helpless, and the victim—a law student—was killed in 1976 for being a member of the reform movement. Solomon himself soon fell foul of the organisation. Within a few years he too had disagreed with Isaias and began calling for internal party democracy. It did little good. By 1980 the pressure on Solomon was intolerable and he fled to Sudan, fearing for his life. The following year he was persuaded to return, but was arrested on arrival, never to be seen again.

Isaias had shown his true colours. Faced with internal challenges he had acted ruthlessly. Always prepared to escalate any disagreement, he had outmanoeuvred his opponents, taking them to a kangaroo court, then torturing them, jailing them, or putting them before a firing squad. His supporters should have learnt from this, but few did. Instead, confronted with the exigencies of a civil war and a fight for independence, they rallied behind their charismatic leader, suppressing concerns about his lack of democratic practices. This is the background to the emergence of the Eritrea People's Liberation Front (EPLF) in 1974–75, which was to lead the country to independence.

While the Eritrean liberation movements fragmented, and then re-formed, they still managed to prosecute the war against the Ethiopians. But they were also involved in bitter struggles against others: effectively an Eritrean civil war. They first erupted in February 1972, when the ELF leaders voted to 'liquidate' the breakaway PLF associated with Isaias and another faction associated with Osman Saleh Sabbe. A truce was negotiated two years later and extended in 1975. By this time the EPLF had emerged and the ELF and EPLF signed an agreement in Khartoum to form a joint command of a United Front.

The pact did not last: the ELF accused the EPLF of opening secret negotiations with the Soviet Union in 1980, which was then allied with the Ethiopian government. In August 1980 the second civil war erupted and the ELF was finally driven from Eritrea, seeking sanctuary in Sudan. The EPLF had won this war and enforced its rule inside the liberated areas, using the old ELF slogan: 'the field cannot tolerate more than one organisation.' Part of the reason for this success was that unlike the ELF, which was fragmented and crippled by rival centres of power, the EPLF tolerated no such divisions. Many were killed in these conflicts and the bitterness this engendered still underlies many of the divisions that exist within Eritrean society today. Nothing has been forgotten and even less has been forgiven, despite the passing of the years.

The EPLF had been born out of the cauldron of a civil conflict, yet within a few years it had managed to establish its supremacy. Foreigners who visited it during the 1980s were struck by what a remarkable movement it was. The EPLF controlled large areas of western Eritrea, bordering on Sudan. The little town of Nakfa remained in its hands throughout the war, although sometimes Ethiopian offensives came close to overwhelming the defences. In this arid, mountainous rear base the EPLF constructed a complex and sophisticated administration. A corner of Eritrea was being transformed into an alternative society, even though it existed under martial conditions.

There were well run hospitals, dug into the hillsides, with rudimentary drugs and saline drips being produced in laboratories. There were workshops that could mend anything from a broken watch to a tank-track. Villagers and nomads had their needs met. Trade was conducted via Sudan, radio transmissions were broadcast and newspapers and magazines produced. Small-scale factories produced plastic sandals beloved of the front line fighters (they were far more appropriate to the conditions than the heavy boots the Ethiopians were equipped with) and sanitary towels for its women.

There had been limited participation by women in the ELF and the EPLF was, at first, a male only organisation. In the early 1970s women began offering to join the movement and the EPLF first opened its ranks and then started actively recruiting female combatants. This was no easy task in a culturally conservative society. To gain the support of local people the EPLF promised they would be like brothers or fathers to the women: there would be no sex in the movement. The rule was strictly enforced: rape was a capital offense and there were stiff punishments for anyone even caught having consensual sex. The strategy worked and women joined in their thousands. After a few years marriage was allowed, with the permission of the unit commander. By 1993 when independence became official, women made up about a third of the roughly 95,000 EPLF fighters.

Women paid as heavy a price for Eritrea's freedom as men. They carried out some of the most dangerous operations behind enemy lines. Sometimes they engaged in 'honey traps'—using sex to gain secrets from Ethiopian officers or luring them to their deaths in such operations. Women served on the front line, to all intents and purposes equal combatants. None, however, gained promotion to the highest ranks in the party during the war. A National Union of Eritrean Women was formed, but it took its orders from the party and enjoyed little autonomy.

When the EPLF was founded Isaias had to share at least some power with others who led the Front. But by the 1980s he had managed to hone it into the movement he wanted. The EPLF was a tough, nationalist organisation that would do the bidding of the leadership. Its members were prepared to make almost any sacrifice for the independence of their country, and frequently laid down their lives. But just as important, it was a broad movement that was in reality controlled by a Leninist inner-party, which took all the most important decisions. It is the manner in which Isaias has worked ever since: maintaining a tight group of utterly loyal lieutenants, whom he shuffles and re-shuffles over time— favouring one over the other, and then reversing course. It may have been a highly successful means of controlling and running a revolutionary movement fighting a much larger enemy—Ethiopia— but it set terrible precedents for a future Eritrea.

Dan Connell identifies the mid 1980s as one of several critical moments in which the seal was set on this process. In a campaign that resembled Mao's Cultural Revolution—which saw key opponents identified, humiliated and eliminated—Isaias launched a 'three privileges campaign'. This coincided with the secretive People's Party holding its second congress in early 1987. The aim, says Connell, was to discredit rival political leaders by appealing over their heads to mid-level cadres, just as Mao had done, and Isaias had witnessed during his time in China:

> That period—the mid-1980s—represents a crucial turning point in the trajectory of the EPRP/EPLF in which Isaias made a bid to marginalise the political core of the movement's founding leadership and then dilute it through the militarisation of party and front decision-making bodies, packing the party's Central Committee and the front's Political Bureau with military men unswervingly loyal to him. The 'three privileges campaign,' which set the stage for this reorganization, was a moral crusade in which Isaias appealed to second-tier cadres to heap shame on their leaders for drinking, womanising and using their positions to secure material advantage. He then brought three generals into both the party CC [Central Committee] and the EPLF's Political Bureau.

If Connell is correct, then this is the decisive moment when Isaias took unquestioned control of the party. But some within the movement are sceptical about this explanation. They point to other debates that would have transformed the EPLF, with serious consideration being given to the establishment of a multi-party system and a mixed economy. Most of the members of the EPLF would have been unaware of just what was going on, since much of this activity took place within the People's Party or the higher echelons of the EPLF. And since secrecy was the hallmark of both organisations, there was little opportunity for open discussion. Instead most fighters concentrated on the task at hand: resisting the onslaught of the Ethiopians and then turning defence into offence.

Of course these were not the only influences that shaped the nature of Eritrea's emerging state. As outlined above, the EPLF's relationship with the movement from which it had been born, the ELF, was important. So too was the constantly conflictual relationship with the TPLF and the long years of warfare with Ethiopia. All had come together to reinforce authoritarian tendencies inside the movement that led the fight for independence. Once this was achieved they would come to the fore.

Independence and beyond

The liberation of Asmara came on 24 May 1991, to the joy of almost every Eritrean. EPLF troops drove into the capital. There were wild celebrations: after decades of struggle the Eritrean people were free to decide their own destiny. There was—for a moment—anticipation that the murderous divisions within Eritrean society would be a thing of the past. Discussions were held with members of the ELF leadership in exile and some began preparing to go home. In the end this did not take place: quite why Isaias changed his mind and did not extend the hand of friendship and reconciliation remains unclear.

This is the recollection of Woldejesus Ammar:

A week after the liberation of Asmara, Issayas declared the formation of the Eritrean Provisional Government in London and saw no need of calling the other factions for participation and power-sharing in a new Eritrea. He disdained the call for a joint Eritrean conference to build national consensus. In his first public speech in Asmara on 20 June 1991, he promised amnesty to all those individuals who were 'duped' by the other factions. He added that any person talking or acting in the name of fronts other than the EPLF will be prosecuted for criminal acts.

Eritreans would be 'forgiven' for backing the 'wrong' movement and allowed to return—but only as individuals. They would not be permitted to come as organisations or movements. Eritrea was to be a one-party state and the EPLF would be that party. This was in stark contrast to the earlier commitments of the EPLF. Its 1977 'National Democratic Programme' had promised an elected leadership, respect for the constitution, equal rights, freedom of speech, worship and peaceful protest. At its Second Congress, held in 1987, the party went further, with a commitment to multi-party politics in the post-independence era. The EPLF promised to: 'Protect the democratic rights of freedom of speech, the press, assembly, worship and peaceful demonstration as well as the right of nationalist political parties and nationalist associations of workers, peasants, women, students, youth and professionals.' Now that independence had been achieved, these promises apparently counted for little.

The political mould of Eritrea had already been determined. Outwardly the Front was a nationalist movement representing all of the country's peoples. In reality it was a tightly run, hierarchical organisation controlled by a narrow clique—the leadership of the People's Party. At its heart was Isaias, who went on to become Eritrea's first president. He was nominally answerable to a National Assembly, but in 1993 it was simply decided that members of the EPLF Central Committee would become members of the Assembly. Isaias was effectively answerable to no one but the inner-circle of the People's Party.

Women, too, were disappointed that their hopes of equality were not borne out in practice. When they entered Asmara and other cities they were full of confidence. As one article from 1993 put it: 'women with long afros and black rubber sandals walk the streets. They have a masculine swagger and their gaze is intense and serious.' Women gradually found themselves back in the home, doing domestic chores. The slogans spoke of 'no development without women's participation,' but the government's practice was rather different. The EPLF, which had once challenged societal mores and even the institution of the family, now embraced both. Victoria Bernal quotes one former fighter as saying: 'We came back from the field and instead of us pulling them forward, they are trying to pull us back... We had changed, but the society had not changed.' This is an all-too familiar story: one that women have endured in almost every conflict across the globe.

The first challenge to Isaias's power came from an unlikely quarter. Civic societies and religious groups, some of which had grown up during the long years of the liberation war, each had a life of their own. For a Leninist this was unacceptable.

The Eritrea Relief Association—the humanitarian wing of the EPLF—had channelled vast sums of money to relieve the suffering of the people since it was founded in 1975. It had won a reputation for efficiency and probity. Both the Eritrean diaspora and the international humanitarian organisations (like Oxfam and Save the Children) had come to know and trust it. Run from Khartoum it had moved vast quantities of aid into the country— particularly during the major famine of 1984–85. Its chairman was Paulos Tesfagiorgis, who came from a well-known Asmara family. Although a member of the EPLF and the People's Party, Paulos was an independent-minded person whose easy charm won him many friends in the international community.

In 1987 the People's Party discussed the future shape of Eritrean society just prior to the EPLF's second congress. Paulos revealed to Gaim Kibreab that he had written a paper for Isaias on the role of civic society associations once freedom had been won. Isaias decided that the issue was 'premature' and—according to Paulos—from then onwards set out to undermine the Relief Association's independence.

In 1991, with the war at an end, Paulos returned home. He went to see Isaias with a proposal to establish a new developmental NGO, the Regional Centre of Human Rights and Development. Paulos says he was encouraged by the meeting; Isaias explained that the country was short of skilled manpower and required a focus on development.

Believing that he had a green light to establish the Centre and participate in rebuilding his country, Paulos filed an application with the Department of the Interior to register the organisation. He was informed that for this to go ahead he would have to promise that the Centre would allow the Department to have full oversight over all its activities. Copies of all correspondence with any foreign organisation would have to be filed with the government. Paulos balked at this interference, but in the end an agreement was reached and the Centre was registered. For a while things went smoothly and in 1994 the Centre was even able to hold a regional development conference. But the party was clearly uncomfortable about the Centre's autonomy and unwilling to allow it to flourish. In late 1994, following several confrontations, the government finally ordered that the Centre should be closed, confiscating its assets. Project money was returned to donors and the initiative was at an end.

If the treatment of the Eritrea Relief Association and the Regional Centre of Human Rights and Development was troubling what happened next was truly alarming. In Eritrea no one is as revered as much as the nation's fighters. The men and women who fought for their country's freedom—many of them paying the ultimate price and being regarded as martyrs—are held in the highest esteem. That, at least, is the official position. How President Isaias actually treated his war veterans tells a rather different story.

In April 1993 the country voted in an internationally supervised referendum on whether to become an independent nation. Some of the polling took place abroad; I helped supervise the London vote. The result was a foregone conclusion: 1,100,260 people (99.83 per cent of the electorate) voted in favour with just 1,822 people voting against. Independence was scheduled to be formally declared on 24 May 1993, two years to the day after the EPLF entered Asmara. But before this could take place the party

1: British encampment near the Ethiopian fortress of Mandala, during the punitive expedition led by Sir Robert Napier to rescue British hostages held by Emperor Tewodros, 1867–68. The force landed South of the Eritrean port of Massawa. [From author's own collection]

ASAB BAY, STRAITS OF BAB-EL-MANDEB—THE FIRST ITALIAN SETTLEMENT IN AFRICA

2: Italian settlement at Assab, in what was to become Italian Eritrea. Engraving in the 28 February 1880 issue of the British weekly *The Graphic*. [Wikimedia Commons]

3: Eritrean troops—or 'Askaris' as they were termed by the Italians—were used in a number of Italian colonial campaigns, including the invasion of Ethiopia in 1935. [From author's own collection]

4: Eritrean Muslim Community club, Asmara, 1946, which preceded the establishment of the Muslim League in early 1947. [From author's own collection]

5: UN Commission visits Eritrea to decide the future of the former Italian colony, 1950. [From author's own collection]

6: Emperor Haile Selassie signs the new constitution of Eritrea incorporating the territory into Ethiopia, but granting it federal status, with considerable autonomy, 1952. [United Press photo from author's collection]

7: Eritrean Liberation Front fighters plant explosives on the railway between the port of Massawa and the capital, Asmara, 1970. [From author's own collection]

8: Eritrean People's Liberation Front fighter with captured Soviet artillery near port of Massawa, 1990. [From author's own collection]

9: Eritrean end user certificate for Bulgarian weapons signed by Eritrea but apparently supplied to the Ogaden National Liberation Front. [UN Monitoring Group report, 2011]

10: Eritrean government demand for two per cent income from Canadian Eritreans plus a defence levy. [UN Monitoring Group report, 2012]

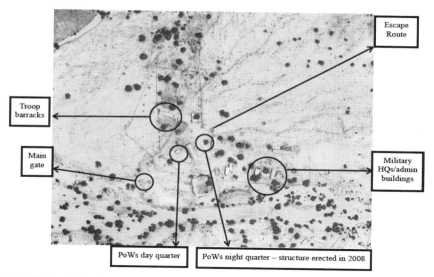

11: Shabay-Mandar, a training camp for Ethiopian armed opposition groups, inside Eritrea. [UN Monitoring Group report, 2012]

12: Eritrean weapons supply depot Kassala, Eastern Sudan. [UN Monitoring Group report, 2014]

13: Eritrean documents found on an Ethiopian opposition fighter, supplied by the Eritrean embassy, South Africa. [UN Monitoring Group report, 2014]

14: Eritrean vigilante group—'Eri-blood'—used to intimidate opposition supporters during the 2014 Bologna festival.

took a number of decisions. Among the most contentious was that its fighters, who had received no pay for the past two years, would have to wait a further four years before being rewarded—irrespective of what job they were given.

This was announced without consultation. On 20 May the troops stationed around Asmara revolted. Many had fought for years—some for decades—for next to no rewards, but now they were in their own capital. Life was expensive and they had responsibilities towards their families. Driving round the city in tanks and armoured cars, the fighters were vociferous in the denunciation of the EPLF leadership, accusing them of abusing their powers. Ministries were occupied and businesses were closed. They demanded that Isaias come to meet them to hear their grievances. While there was plenty of anger there was no suggestion of a coup: this was a protest and nothing more.

The president met the fighters and was ordered by them to walk to Asmara Stadium to speak to the troops, who were ferried in by bus and truck. With the stadium packed to capacity with well-armed fighters, the president listened to their demands before assuring them that he had sympathy for what they had to say. He promised that US$7 million would be allocated to their most pressing needs and that a commission of inquiry would be held to look into their wider allegations of abuse of power and corruption. He also promised to convene a third congress of the EPLF. By 7:00 p.m. Isaias had accepted all their demands and the disgruntled troops agreed to return to their barracks. It proved to be a costly mistake. Once safely in his office the president went on the air to attack the soldiers as 'illegal, misguided and infantile'. Over the coming months between 200 and 300 were rounded up and imprisoned at Adi Qala—Eritrea's most notorious prison. There they rotted for the next two years before being sentenced to up to twelve years in prison.

The treatment of the wounded and disabled fighters was equally severe. During the war the EPLF had done its best to look after its wounded and maimed combatants, even when it was fighting in the field, with few resources to spare for their care. The main hospital at Orota performed surgical miracles to reconstruct their shattered bodies in wards driven deep into the hillsides to avoid Ethiopian bombs. So one might have assumed that in 1993, once the war was over, the government would have welcomed the formation of an Eritrean War Disabled Fighters' Association. A rehabilitation centre was established at Mai Habar, a few miles outside the capital. It was prepared to receive 3,000 veterans, but over 10,000 arrived and the centre was overwhelmed. To make matters worse the president refused all outside help—whether offered from international organisations or the diaspora.

In 1994 the Association called for a meeting with Isaias, but he was unwilling to grant this request. So, on 11 July that year the disabled veterans marched on the capital, despite being told that permission for the demonstration had been refused. They set off anyway and were met by police and told to disperse. Others might have turned around but the ex-fighters were made of sterner stuff and refused. Some threw stones at the police, who replied by firing live rounds at the crowd. Some of the demonstrators were killed. When the news reached the capital there was astonishment and outrage that these esteemed liberation heroes should be treated this way. Rumours circulated that a massacre had taken place. The president's response was dismissive: 'We cannot afford to slaughter sheep for you every morning,' he is said to have remarked.

The treatment of the Eritrean Relief Association and the veterans and disabled combatants became the blueprint for Isaias's response to the requests from a range of other civic organisations. Women who had fought for their country, religious organisations—Christian and Muslim—and the students of Asmara University all suffered a similar fate. The president was simply not prepared to brook any opposition. Indeed, it soon became clear that he was unwilling to tolerate the establishment of any organisation that was in any way independent of the EPLF. Every group had to be dependent on the party and finally on the president and those he gathered around himself.

Towards repression

Despite these disturbing events many Eritreans, as well as the country's small band of international supporters, hoped that these were just early difficulties that would be resolved over time. Few believed they were the hallmark of a truly repressive regime. And for a while the evidence seemed to bear this out. Eritrea took its place on the world stage, joining the UN and the African Union. Relations with Ethiopia improved and were normalised. At home a small but lively independent press emerged, sometimes even carrying material critical of the government. The BBC and Reuters were among international news organisations that stationed correspondents in the country.

Eritrea was born a one-party state. When the Provisional Government took power in 1991 it banned all parties other than the EPLF. Members of other parties could only return to the country as individuals. As Isaias put it in a speech in Asmara Stadium marking Martyrs' Day, 20 June, Eritrea would not become a 'playground of political organisations.' The democracy Eritreans had fought for was proving elusive. But at least a start was made on drawing up a constitution. Proclamation No. 1 issued by the Provisional Government called for the drafting of a constitution 'on the basis of which a democratic order would be established.' The task was given to Bereket Habte Selassie. A commission was established with a two year mandate to consult as widely as possible on what the constitution should contain.

A first draft was ready by 1995. There was extensive public discussion followed by revisions. The final draft was submitted to the National Assembly in July 1996 and ratified in May 1997. The constitution contained guarantees of all sorts of human rights—including free speech, assembly and an independent judiciary.

All that was required was for the document to be implemented. For a moment it seemed that this was about to occur. The 1997 presidential dinner (the most prestigious annual reception) held on the eve of Independence Day, was dedicated to the Constitution. On Independence Day itself, 24 May, during the celebration in the national stadium a copy of the Constitution was carried from one end of the arena to the other, and presented to Isaias. The moment was of enormous symbolic importance. A committee to frame election laws was formed and a draft was submitted to the National Assembly for discussion. Then fate took a hand. In May 1998 the border war with Ethiopia erupted, and the constitution was set to one side.

When the war ended two years later the issue was back on the agenda. In September 2000 the National Assembly passed a resolution calling for general elections to be held before the end of 2001. The task of bringing this about fell to Mahmoud Sherifo, the Minister of Regional Government. He completed a draft law on political parties and was about to start public consultations when the president ordered him to cease and report to him. The minister refused, arguing that his mandate came from the National Assembly. Isaias promptly dismissed him. Since then the Constitution—despite being ratified—has gathered dust. In May 2014 the president finally put the matter to rest: a new constitution would be drafted based on what Isaias described as important lessons gleaned from 'hostile external schemes aimed at derailing the nation-building process.' There is little evidence of progress since this announcement.

By 2001 matters were coming to a head, as even some of Isaias's closest confidants understood that the situation could not be allowed to fester any longer. The first rumours of dissent came during the border war of 1998–2000. Eritrean fighters, once famed for their ability to win against overwhelming odds, had been routed. Andebrhan Welde Giorgis, once close to Isaias, says that the reverses 'shattered the aura of invincibility' of the army and 'exposed the structural weaknesses in the Eritrean operational command and military intelligence, and raised the spectre of further setbacks.' Part of the blame, it was being whispered, lay with the president himself. Isaias was said to have intervened directly in the strategic decisions, giving orders rather than allowing the military to use their judgement on how best to run the war. Some of the old hands in the military who had been frozen out of positions of influence returned to their posts. With their help—it is said—a full-scale defeat was avoided.

Exactly what took place is still not clear, but Haile Wold'ensae explained to Dan Connell that amid the chaos of war the issue of Isaias stepping down was discussed. The president's supporters accuse his critics of passing to Ethiopian officials an offer to remove Isaias, via American and Italian intermediaries. They suggest that a full-scale coup plot was under way. The president's critics were labelled 'traitors' when the inevitable recriminations got under way.

Andebrhan cites as significant a central committee meeting of the ruling party (by this time renamed the PFDJ) that was held from 31 August until 2 September 2000:

> This marked the first ever overt conversation that generated a historical debate within the historical leadership of the EPLF... The president faced concrete, direct and substantive criticism, accusing him of mismanaging the affairs of state and displaying an increasingly autocratic style of leadership. Put on the defensive and unable to present a coherent and credible justification of his conduct and actions, the president resorted to subterfuge and blackmail to muzzle the debate. With the Rubicon crossed, however, there was no turning back.

The September meeting of the National Assembly discussed the president's conduct of the border war and established a commission to assess what had taken place and to draw up rules for multi-party elections to be held in December 2001. When pushed on why he had failed to hold regular meetings of the party and the government, the president retorted simply: 'it was not convenient to convene meetings.' Frustrated by his stance senior officials began collecting signatures for a petition calling for regular meetings of the Front and the National Assembly. The president and his supporters retaliated by spreading allegations of betrayal. The scene was set for a final showdown.

The first open revolt came in September 2000. A group of prominent intellectuals—thirteen in total—came together in Berlin. They signed a letter to the president demanding greater transparency and freedom of expression and questioning the causes of the recent 'tragic war' with Ethiopia. The signatories included Paulos Tesfagiorgis (the only one still inside Eritrea) and others—like Bereket Habte Selassie who had drafted the constitution and Kassahun Checole, a well known publisher—who were living abroad. The 'Berlin Manifesto', which was leaked to the media, caused a stir in Eritrean circles, but no change in government policy.

In May 2001 a group of fifteen of the EPLF's most senior members published an open letter to party members. Soon known as the 'G15' they included men and women who had fought for their country's independence for decades. In it they accused Isaias of stifling debate and damaging the country. The letter called for human rights, an independent judiciary and the establishment of a 'constitutional government through free and fair elections.' The signatories included Mahmoud Sherifo, Minister of Local Government and effectively Isaias's deputy, Haile Wold'ensae, Minister of Foreign Affairs and then Trade and Industry, and Mesfin Hagos, the former Chief of Staff of the Eritrean Defence Force. Over the next few months the dissidents gave interviews to local and international media expanding on and explaining their criticisms.

FROM FREEDOM TO DICTATORSHIP

It was a challenge Isaias could not ignore, and his critics probably knew what was coming. Why they failed to take pre-emptive action between May and September is something of a conundrum: perhaps they were transfixed by the threat they faced, rather like rabbits in headlights. On 18 and 19 September 2001 the axe fell. In dawn raids the president sent his security forces to round up eleven of the fifteen signatories. Of the remaining original signatories three were not in the country and one had been persuaded to withdraw his support. The prisoners were first held at a naval base and then transferred to the newly constructed Eiraeiro prison on the coastal plain, north of the Asmara-Massawa road. None has been ever seen again; some are reported to have died in detention. They have faced no trials or tribunals and their fate can only be surmised. The only explanation given by the authorities was that the signatories had 'committed crimes against the sovereignty, security and peace of the nation.'

The repression did not end there. Even before the arrests of his closest colleagues the president had moved against students at the University of Asmara. Around 400 were rounded up after they demonstrated to free one of their leaders in August 2001. They were held in a desert detention camp South of Massawa. At least two were feared to have died of heat and dehydration. The university itself was closed and students transferred to vocational schools in military camps.

On 18 September, at the same time as members of the G15 were being arrested, the government shut down all private newspapers and publications. The date was no accident—coming less than a week after al-Qaeda's attacks on New York and Washington. The world's attention was focussed on the collapse of the Twin Towers and the passenger aircraft crashing into the Pentagon. There was little interest in events in Eritrea. President Isaias went on French radio to denounce thirteen editors and journalists who had been rounded up: they were, he said, traitors. 'These are not even journalists,' he declared. 'You cannot say a spy is a journalist.' Nor was this the end of the clampdown. In November 2006 another wave of arrests saw journalists from the state media jailed. A group of elders who attempted to mediate between the president and his critics was also detained; some never emerged from custody. Today the country is at the very bottom of the Reporters Without Borders annual league tables ranking press freedom around the world. Eritrea ranks at number 180 on the list—just below North Korea and Turkmenistan.

President Isaias—challenged by those who had fought alongside him for so many years—had emerged victorious. He now ruled supreme, surrounded by a small clique of party, military and security officials, none of whom was his equal.

At the same time blame for the current predicament cannot be laid solely at the feet of Isaias. His colleagues in the EPLF leadership must take their share of the responsibility for the country's predicament. The problem for them was that he was not just clever and manipulative; Isaias was far more ruthless than any of his contemporaries. He was prepared to use any means to hang onto power and had no compunction about destroying anyone who questioned his authority. As one former fighter put it: 'He uses and disposes of human beings as if they were plastic shopping bags.'

UN Commission of Inquiry

International concern about Eritrea's human rights abuses has gradually increased. Amnesty International and Human Rights Watch have produced regular reports outlining the repression of anyone who fell out with the regime, from politicians and journalists to religious leaders. In July 2014 the UN's Human Rights Council agreed to establish a Commission of Inquiry to report on the situation. The resolution provided a long list of alleged abuses that it asked a Special Rapporteur to report on. The report called upon the Eritrean government: 'to cooperate fully with the Special Rapporteur and the commission of inquiry, to permit them and their staff members unrestricted access to visit the country, to give due consideration to the recommendations contained in the reports of the Special Rapporteur, and to provide them with the information necessary for the fulfilment of their mandates', underlining 'the importance for all States to lend their support to the Special Rapporteur and the commission of inquiry for the discharge of their mandates.'

The establishment of a UN Commission of Inquiry was something of a rarity. Previous Commissions had investigated North Korea, Syria and Burundi. The Eritrea Commission was chaired by Mike Smith, Professor in the Department of Policing, Intelligence and Counter-Terrorism at Macquarie University in New South Wales, Australia. He was supported by Sheila B. Keetharuth, a human rights lawyer from Mauritius and Victor Dankwa, a Ghanaian constitutional expert. Although they contacted the Eritrean government repeatedly they received little in the way of co-operation. Instead of visiting Eritrea and taking evidence the Commission was forced to tour the diaspora, talking to as many sources as they could find. They visited the refugee camps in Ethiopia as well as speaking to exiles around the world. The result of their investigation was a damning 483-page report based on 550 interviews and 160 written submissions.

Presenting their findings in June 2015, Mike Smith gave this assessment:

A massive domestic surveillance network penetrates all levels of society, turning even family members against each other. Much of the population is subject to forced conscription and labour, sometimes in slave-like conditions. Tens of thousands have been imprisoned, often without charge and for indeterminate periods... Over the past several months, our Commission of Inquiry has found that systematic, widespread, and gross human rights violations have been and are still being committed with impunity in Eritrea.

Our findings are sobering. The many violations in Eritrea are of a scope and scale seldom seen anywhere else in today's world. Basic freedoms are curtailed, from movement to expression; from religion to association. The Commission finds that crimes against humanity may have occurred with regard to torture, extrajudicial executions, forced labour and in the context of national service.

The last sentence proved particularly significant. The UN Human Rights Council asked the Commissioners to continue their work for a further year and to report on whether there had—indeed—been 'crimes against humanity.' Such a finding would be among the most serious charges that could be laid against a state. A year later the Commission reported once more. Their verdict was clear. The Commissioners reported that Eritrean officials had committed 'crimes of enslavement, imprisonment, enforced disappearance, torture, reprisals as other inhuman acts, persecution, rape and murder.' They concluded that: 'there are reasonable grounds to believe that crimes against humanity have been committed in Eritrea since 1991.'

The Eritrean government was furious. By 2016 President Isaias had authorised his officials to try to break out of the isolation in which they found themselves. They did all they could to discredit the Commission of Inquiry. The Eritrean Ministry of Foreign Affairs issued a statement accusing the Commission of showing a 'total disregard for the basic principles of fundamental rules of procedure and established norms of fair play' and suggesting that its credibility has been undermined. The statement failed to mention that it was the government's own actions that kept the Commission out of Eritrea.

Documents leaked from the Eritrean capital provided an insight into the scale of the official campaign against the Commission. The government's aim was to collect 300,000 signatures protesting against the work of the Commission. A seven-page letter in Tigrinya from the Ministry of Foreign Affairs detailed the operation. Every Eritrean foreign embassy is required to fulfil an allocated quota of signatures against the Commission's report. For Eritreans in the diaspora this was not a mere request. Living—as many of them do—in countries like Sudan, they were open to real pressure to comply with this request for support. Refusal would leave the exiles open to accusations of being unpatriotic, resulting in a denial of assistance from any Eritrean embassy—including passports, visas or any other form of official documentation or permission. Thousands of Eritreans across the diaspora were officially encouraged to travel to Geneva. 'Spontaneous' protests were planned against the Commission's findings, even before they had been made public. In the event there were competing demonstrations when the findings were revealed in Geneva in June 2016. Critics of the Eritrean government among the diaspora also came in their thousands and—according to the Swiss police—outnumbered the pro-government demonstrations.

When the second report came before the UN Human Rights Council in July 2016 the Eritrean authorities fought a rear-guard action to try to prevent it being adopted. President Isaias's senior aid, Yemane Ghebreab, called for the report to be rejected, claiming that it would stoke tensions across the Horn. 'Its grave consequences will not be limited to Eritrea but will engulf the entire region,' he said. 'This resolution will be used and abused to fan the flames of war.'

In the event, the text was somewhat watered down, following objections from several countries, including China and the United States. Earlier drafts explicitly called for it to be referred to the Security Council. Instead it was sent to all 'relevant organs of the UN for consideration and urgent action.' Speaking for the Commission, Mike Smith welcomed the decision saying that it 'fully endorses the work we have done over the past two years.' Eritrea was recommended to be referred to the International Criminal Court and the Special Rapporteur was given a mandate to examine human rights in the country for a further year.

* * *

The adoption of the Commission of Inquiry's report was a considerable blow to the regime. It had mobilised all its resources to try and defeat it, without success. Its finding that crimes against humanity had, indeed, been committed by the authorities against their own people was also a setback from those in the EU who were attempting to establish a new relationship with Asmara to try to halt the exodus of refugees. A close relationship with a regime with this appellation will be difficult for any western state with a commitment to human rights.

Much depends on how President Isaias and his associates respond. The regime is not easy to second-guess. Outsiders have long attempted to get to grips with the president. On 12 November 2008 the American Ambassador to Asmara, Ronald K. McMullen, sent a secret cable to the US State Department, entitled: 'Is Isaias Unhinged.' It contained a not very flattering, but perceptive, biography of the president. Its conclusions cannot—for obvious reasons—be verified, but it is worth reproducing and is carried in full at the end of this book. [See Appendix 2.] But the key point he made is this: Isaias is 'an austere and narcissistic dictator whose political ballast derives from Maoist ideology fine-tuned during Eritrea's thirty-year war for independence.' Furthermore, he was said to harbour 'paranoid beliefs' that the United States and the Ethiopians are attempting to assassinate him.

This is the individual who controls the destiny of Eritrea and whose decisions, as we have seen, have serious implications for the rest of the Horn of Africa and the Arabian peninsula. No wonder he has managed to remain president while being loathed and feared by large sections of his own people. Many have underestimated Isaias Afewerki: no one has found a means of ending his rule.

7

ERITREA'S ECONOMY

SMOKE AND MIRRORS

The Eritrean economy is not what it seems. Eritrea appears to be a poor, developing country, with most of its citizens working in peasant agriculture while the state relies for its hard currency on a small but growing mining sector and remittance income from the diaspora. In part this is accurate, hence Eritrea differs little from many other African states. Its GDP per capita is somewhere below Guinea in West Africa, and just above Mozambique in Southern Africa. How anyone can be certain is hard to fathom— as we shall see—but as a generality this is probably accurate, as far as it goes.

There is, however, another dominant reality. Eritrea's economy, like its politics, has been captured by a narrow elite. Alongside the open, observable economy there is another, much more significant, hidden economy. This is entirely controlled by the party and—ultimately—by President Isaias himself. The officials around him do not just muddle through: they have a reputation for being efficient and organised, using long term planning to achieve the aims of the president and the party.

The scale of this second reality has been spelled out in detail over several years by the UN Monitoring Group, but few outside of the Security Council have paid much attention. These observations are from the Monitor's 2015 report. They complain that their work has been hampered by a lack of financial transparency across all aspects of economic life. This quotation gives a flavour of what is really going on: 'Senior officials within the Government and PFDJ continue to exert full economic control over revenue through a clandestine network of State-owned companies.' The UN believes that these activities, directed by the most senior government and military officials, operate not only inside Eritrea but also abroad. They will be outlined below.

This assessment, corroborated by independent information, indicates that the covert economy is far more important than the overt economy. Yet this clandestine public face of Eritrea is not—for the most part—reflected in reports prepared by international organisations, including the IMF, World Bank, African Development Bank etc. Let us begin with the picture that is painted by these official bodies.

Eritrea's overt economy

The African Development Bank provides a pithy summary of the economy's growth in its 2015 report: 'Economic growth is projected at 2.1% in 2015, up from 1.3% in 2013 and 2% in 2014, reflecting improved economic activity and increased investment in the mining sector.'

The key question is this: how does the African Development Bank know? As the UN Monitors spell out, the Eritrean government has never published a budget, so how can the Bank publish such an assessment? The answer is—almost certainly—that their economists have been provided with limited information that the state wishes to release. It is a kind of 'take it or leave it' relationship, with little opportunity for a forensic audit or a deeper scrutiny.

Nor is this just a financial question. The UN Commission of Inquiry into Human Rights in Eritrea pointed out that there has never been a census of the country's population. The Commission therefore comes to this conclusion: 'In the absence of an official census, Eritrean population is estimated in-between 3.2 and 6.5 million.'

Others use different statistics. Perhaps the most authoritative finding was from a report dated March 1997, from Eritrea's National Statistics Office, Department of Macro Policy and International Economic Co-operation and the Office of the President. Entitled 'Eritrea Demographic and Health Survey, 1995', it states: 'Since there has not been any survey or census conducted in the country before or after independence, the population size is not known with any degree of precision. Some rough professional estimates put the country's population in the range of 2.5 to 3.5 million. Estimates of the number of Eritreans living abroad range between 700,000 and 1,000,000.'

Outside organisations have provided other statistics. The African Development Bank states: 'As of 2014, the population was estimated at 3.5 million', and quotes the 'National Statistical Office, 2014.' By contrast the CIA World Factbook put the figure at 6,527,689—a July 2015 estimate. The Eritrea-European Union Co-operation Agreement, signed in Asmara on 28 January 2016, carries this assessment: 'In statistical reports, population size varies from 3.5 to 6.5 mio [sic] people, owing to the fact that no recent census date is available. Related figures (i.e. GDP per capita) thus also have to be assessed with caution.'

Pause for a moment and consider what this implies. If the population estimates are so widely different and there is no published budget, how can almost any development indicator be trusted? As the EU Co-operation Agreement signed with the Eritrean government puts it diplomatically, all related data must be 'assessed with caution.' Growth rates per capita could be wildly incorrect. Eritrea's celebrated successes in reducing maternal mortality could be completely skewed. Its percentage of pupils in school may be little more than fiction. No one can be really sure; no official report can be relied upon in this respect—all are based on a quicksand of estimates, guesses and official briefings.

This is not just a statistical problem. Consider the African Development Bank statement in 2015: 'Eritrea is aiming at creating a modern, private sector-led economy.' Where does the Bank get this from? It is quoting the government's policy document, issued two decades earlier (1994) together with a later 'National Indicative Development Plan.' In other words, the Bank is simply reflecting what the Eritrean authorities have told it. There is little sign of any independent investigation or probing of the evidence. This assessment that the government aims to create a 'modern, private sector-led economy' is not supported by the European Union. The EU's joint report with the Eritrean government states: 'Private sector engagement is not yet fully complementary to the Government of the State of Eritrea's development initiatives.' As we will see, the EU's cautious statement is somewhat more accurate—yet even this polite formulation hides what is really going on.

The Eritrean growth tables provided by the Bank are similarly questionable. They show that for the past three years they are based on little more than informed thumb-sucking. The last confirmed growth figure the Bank can quote (and what is the source?) dates from 2013. The figure for 2014 is an estimate and the figure for 2015 is a projection. These are hardly solid grounds for any report. The Eritrea-EU Co-operation Agreement has, as one of its stated objectives, an improvement in the production of government statistics by the Office of the Auditor General, which is described as the country's 'Supreme Audit Institution.' It would be encouraging to know that this would really take place, but if past practice is anything to go by it is unlikely to bear fruit: transparency is hardly a hallmark of President Isaias's government.

Agriculture

Agriculture is mainly peasant-based, with most farmers barely making a living. The African Development Bank states: 'Based on anecdotal evidence, poverty is still widespread in the country where 65 per cent of the population lives in rural areas and 80 per cent depend on subsistence agriculture for their livelihoods.' In a year of good agricultural production, the country can produce a maximum of 70–80 per cent of its cereal requirements and in a bad year, as little as 20–30 per cent. This puts the country and its people at real, and continuing, risk.

A joint mission organised by two specialised UN agencies, the Food and Agriculture Organisation (FAO) and World Food Programme (WFP), produced a report in 2005 that provides perhaps the best insight into why agriculture absorbs such a large proportion of the population, yet provides so little output. As they put it: 'Agriculture is the most vital sector in Eritrea despite a rather small estimated contribution of only 12–15 per cent to national GDP. The crop and livestock sectors together employ the vast majority of the population and provide the basis for food security. However, domestic food production even in good years remains well below the requirements, and the country relies heavily on commercial imports and food aid.' Eritrea is almost at the very bottom of the 2015 UNDP's 2015 Human Development Index. Only the Central African Republic and Niger come lower.

Why is output so low?

Geography has a good deal to do with it. Rainfall is erratic, soil is poor and there are no perennial rivers, making irrigation difficult. But this is not the whole story. Labour is very scarce as a result of conscription. As the FAO and WFP say: 'The shortage of labour was observed everywhere. The main cause of this shortage is the conscription of men into defence forces and national service for long periods of time. The army does provide assistance in crop harvesting and threshing, but the extent of this assistance was difficult to ascertain.' The unresolved tensions with Ethiopia following the border war—and the president's insistence on maintaining high alert in a state of 'no war-no peace'—have drained the economy of its manpower. The rural areas have been particularly hard hit, as there are few mechanisms to escape conscription. This is not the only area in which conscription has a negative impact. The Ethiopia-Eritrea border is closed. Traditional trading routes and traditional pastures are denied to farmers, again cutting output. This has hit hard the Eritrean ports of Massawa and Assab, which once handled almost all Ethiopian trade. Today they lie largely idle, with Ethiopia having diverted its imports and exports through Dijbouti.

The cumulative impact of these issues has been felt across the population and poverty is widespread. 'Poverty is still rampant,' noted the FAO/WFP. 'A study undertaken in 2002/03 indicates that 66 per cent of the population has incomes below the poverty line (and 37 per cent below the extreme poverty line). On average 66 per cent of household expenditure is spent on food in urban areas, and 71 per cent in rural areas.'

The result is severe malnutrition. A World Health Organisation study in 2010 concluded that half of all Eritrean children are stunted as a result of malnutrition. The worst time for these children is when they stop breastfeeding. Then the rate of what the WHO describes as 'chronic malnutrition' rises to 71 per cent. Meanwhile the prices of basic commodities have careered upwards. By mid-2016 a kilo of sugar cost the equivalent of €1.80 and a kilo of potatoes €2.00.

ERITREA'S ECONOMY

Formal employment

This consists of substantial but poorly paid government employment, and a private sector described by the African Development Bank as 'small and underdeveloped'. Apart from these there is really only one major development. That is the Nevsun mine at Bisha, 150 km west of Asmara. The mine is controversial, with accusations that it has employed government conscripts. It is an accusation hotly contested by the Canadian mining company which part owns the mine, along with the government. Nevsun has a 60 per cent stake in the venture, with the Eritrean state holding the remaining 40 per cent. The prospects of the mine appear good. Having initially produced gold it has subsequently moved onto copper and Nevsun says there are large deposits of zinc to be exploited. Three other companies—two Chinese and one Australian—are currently involved in mining projects, but Nevsun's is the only mine that is currently operational.

Work at Bisha began in September 2008 and Nevsun hired Senet, a South African company, to undertake the construction of the infrastructure. The work was subcontracted to an Eritrean company, Segen. This is what the UN Commission of Inquiry had to say: 'Even though BMSC [Bisha Mining Shareholders Corporation] and Senet were able to directly employ foreign workers and some Eritreans who had been released to perform technical and skilled functions, they were required by the Eritrean Government to hire Segen and other Eritrean public companies to carry out all of the unskilled labour and basic construction work.'

The UN Commission found that Senet attempted to conceal the status of the workforce, most of whom were National Service conscripts. One former conscript described how his unit came to work at the mine:

In February 2010, we all had to go to Bisha. We did not get any details, we were only told to go to Bisha. I don't know how many we were, but it was the whole military division. I was part of a team to do construction, we were building houses. They kept us working in the construction site. They would not tell us what we were doing, but sometimes we heard we were building the offices or living or changing quarters. We just guessed what it was for.

Most of the superiors came with us. We were under the control of our direct commanding officers; the commanding officer of the brigade gave orders to our superiors. Before we went to Bisha, they briefed us that we were not to reveal our identity as soldiers. We wore civilian clothes and working uniforms.

In my company, Segen, there were Eritreans and Indians. In Mereb and Senet, there were different nationalities, including white people, many Eritreans and foreigners. We were not allowed to talk to them. The structure at the mine was hard to understand. They kept it that way deliberately.

However, after talking among us, we understood that the agreement between the Segen CEO and our commanders was that Segen would pay $21 per day per worker, but we only received 450 Nakfa per month [approximately $30]. I think there was an official agreement and an informal agreement. We continued our life, as in the military base, the salary was paid by the officers.

The UN Commission report contains many statements detailing the brutal conditions under which these conscripts worked. In November 2014 three Eritreans brought a lawsuit against Nevsun in Canada, accusing the company of using forced labour. This case is slowly making its way through the Canadian courts.

The Bisha mine is one of the chief sources of income and hard currency for the Eritrean government. The UN Commission found that Nevsun had paid the Eritrean authorities $85 million in royalties and taxes and would contribute an estimated $14 billion over the next ten years. The UN Monitors, using published company reports, concluded that Nevsun has paid rather more. They calculate that since 2011 the company has paid close to $528 million in income taxes, royalties and other government remittances to the Government, $226 million to the Eritrean National Mining Corporation (ENAMCO), which owns 40 per cent of the mine, in the form of dividends and $299 million in local supply of goods and services. Exactly what proportion of the government's revenue this represents is impossible to say, since no budget has been published. The African Development Bank report, dated 2015, could only quote statistics from three years earlier, before the Bisha mine came on stream. At that time there was no mining.

Prospects for mineral extraction are said to be good. A second mine, producing gold, is reported to have begun commercial extraction at Koka in 2016. It is 60 per cent owned by a subsidiary of China's Shanghai Construction Group. The Colluli potash project, which is owned by the Australian company Danakali, is projected to begin production in 2018. The mine is in the Danakil Depression, one of the hottest and lowest points on earth, and is reported to have reserves of 6 billion tonnes of potassium-bearing salts. A number of European and Asian companies are also reported to be investigating the country's potential. The Eritrean government gave this upbeat assessment in December 2015. 'Recently, commercial quantity of oil and gas reserve [sic] has been confirmed. Even though the country's full potential has not been exploited fully, it is reported that it has a potential of producing to 200,000 barrels of oil per day.'

The question is whether these prospects will be realised. It is worth noting that Eritrea is one of the most difficult countries for business to operate in anywhere in the world. The country comes 184th out of 189 in the World Bank's 2016 'Doing Business' index. It is not hard to see why. Many regulations are non-existent. Essential supplies are difficult to come by, with 180 interruptions of supply a year. Businesses are left with power for around 270 days a year. Most have to turn to their own generators, assuming they can find diesel to power them. Hardly surprising then that Eritrea's growth rate has stagnated.

The overall situation is well summarised by the US State Department in its 2015 'Investment Climate' Statement.

The investment climate in Eritrea is not conducive to U.S. investment. While there is opportunity, especially in the extractive industries sector, the Government of the State of Eritrea (GSE) maintains a command economy, with government activities predominating over private enterprise. Unreliable power, complicated and changing import regulations, difficult air and ground transportation links, insufficient port facilities, lack of fuel, unrealistic exchange rate, restrictions on repatriation of profits, the near impossibility of getting a construction permit unless the project is government-sanctioned, and in-country travel restrictions all work to undermine trade and investment.

One needs to add one note of caution. It is quite possible that major investors, like Nevsun, have private arrangements with the authorities that circumvent these regulations. They may well also have permission to bring in their own fuel and other supplies, without having to cope with the red tape that bedevils smaller businesses.

In November 2015 it was announced that new notes would replace the previous currency. The population was given six weeks to redeem the old Nakfa notes for new ones at par—that is one old note for one new note. On the face of it this was a neutral act. In reality it was designed to destroy all the currency that had been secretly hoarded by businesses and private citizens. At a stroke the wealth of many people, carefully saved over the years, was wiped out. The hoards of notes were frequently the result of irregular or covert currency transactions and their owners had no way of explaining how they had accumulated the money. In the end some people simply gave the old currency away—or abandoned it with the rubbish. In the wake of the announcement no more than 5,000 Nakfa could be withdrawn from bank accounts a month—even if it had been deposited legally. Any larger sums required special authorisation. To pay for a wedding celebration, for example, an application must be made to the Commercial Bank of Eritrea declaring every single item to be purchased. A letter from the local authorities is required to verify the celebration. Nothing—it seems—is spared the invasive scrutiny of the Eritrean bureaucracy.

The covert economy

The controlling forces that drive the Eritrean economy are hidden. As the UN Monitors put it in their 2015 report:

> The Government continues not to disclose its budget appropriations and the country's budget is not publicly available. In general, financial transparency also leads to financial accountability, which requires Governments to justify raising public resources and revenue and to explain how they are used. The standard practice by institutions and Governments alike to build and maintain budgets in order to demonstrate compliance with laws and communicate effectiveness is a practice not currently followed in Eritrea.

This is the way President Isaias operates. Former officials say that it is not a question of budgets not being published—none exists, even inside the Treasury. Kubrom Hosabay, who was Chief of the Treasury and then Chief of the Inland Revenue until 2006, says that no formal budget appropriation takes place even inside ministries. No budget document was drawn up, even discreetly, to which officials within government could refer. Only recurrent expenditure is tracked, with expenses like salaries, utilities and stationery budgeted for, but no formal budgets are drawn up. These are simply copied from the preceding year.

In their 2014 report the UN Monitors spelled out how the covert economy really functions. The UN had: 'obtained information through direct sources that Government officials have created and maintain a global financial structure that is not registered in the name of PFDJ. This architecture includes tax havens, secret trusts and companies incorporated under the names of officials and, in most cases, under the names of private individuals.' This conclusion was reinforced the following year: 'The complete lack of financial transparency by the Government of Eritrea enables it to maintain a PFDJ-controlled informal economy.'

As the Monitors have repeatedly informed the UN Security Council, most companies in Eritrea are owned by the state and managed by senior government officials, the PFDJ and the military. 'The network of companies linked to PFDJ continues to be the driving force of the economy. The Government, through PFDJ and the military, has exclusive control of all economic activity, including the agriculture, trade and production sectors,' the Monitors reported in 2015.

How did this informal economy come about? This goes back to the legacy of the country's fight for independence. In its 2011 report Monitors said:

> The informal, PFDJ-controlled economy is in many respects a legacy of the financial organization of EPLF during the liberation struggle. It involves a much higher proportion of hard currency transactions than the formal economy and is managed almost entirely offshore through a labyrinthine multinational network of companies, individuals and bank accounts, many of which do not declare any affiliation to PFDJ or the Eritrean State, and routinely engage in 'grey' or illicit activities.

It is, of course, impossible to accurately assess quite how large this informal or covert economy is, but one can sketch an outline of its relative significance. Certain key elements of the economic structure are relevant. These include the Red Sea Trading Corporation and other business ventures owned by the ruling party and the various means by which the regime extracts funds from its large diaspora. The Red Sea Trading Corporation (RSTC) was established during the 1980s. Its initial funds were reported to be just $20,000. After independence it might have been disbanded, but instead it was maintained. The Red Sea Trading Corporation blossomed with the regime's support. Over the next decade it became part of a network of firms that came to dominate the economy. These exist under an umbrella: the Hidri Trust Fund, which is run by the Economic Affairs Department of the PFDJ, and headed by Hagos Gebrihiwot 'Kisha'. There are some thirty front companies, run by the ruling party, with a net worth estimated to be in the order of $500 million. The Red Sea Trading Corporation is arguably the biggest of the PFDJ's commercial operations, but every company specialises in one activity: RSTC specialises in imports and distribution of commodities and commercial goods. Other companies are government fronts. Everything from Asmara's only five-star hotel (the Asmara Palace Hotel—formerly the Intercontinental) to internet cafes, publishing houses, insurance companies and bookshops are owned by a PFDJ run company or government department.

The initial aim was to hold down the costs of basic commodities and to channel profits into a fund to assist crippled veterans of the war and their families, but there is no evidence that this has been done. The head of the tax system, Brigadier General Estifanos Seyoum, in 2001 accused the RSTC of not paying its share of taxes. He had a Master's degree in Finance and Economics from the University of Wisconsin–Madison, and therefore had a strong background to make such a judgement. Estifanos soon paid a price for challenging the Corporation. He was removed from his position and imprisoned, providing a graphic illustration of just how powerful the conglomerate and its controllers really are.

The main hubs through which the Eritrean state operates are Dubai and Qatar. Dubai serves as a conduit for the regime and a route for many of its international operations. In their 2011 report the UN Monitors provided a case study of how this worked. This was carried in detail in the section on 'Arabian friends' in Chapter 5. What this indicates is Dubai's role as a banking nexus through which PFDJ offshore finances flow, controlled by trusted party cadres. The funds are then available to senior Eritrean officers who travel through Dubai en route to other countries. Among them is the Commander of the Air Force, Teklai Habteselassie, who is one of President Isaias's most trusted officers. He was recorded travelling via Dubai to Ukraine in December 2009 to procure arms.

The control of foreign currency is said to be overseen by Hagos Gebrehiwot Maesho, who runs what is described as a 'hard currency oversight board' that decides how much to allocate for key foreign purchases, including arms supplies. In the past these purchases have been—at least in part—financed by donations from Libya (before the overthrow of Colonel Gaddafi) and Qatar. In 2011 the UN Monitors reported that: 'Qatar is perhaps Eritrea's most important economic partner at the moment, and Qatari officials have acknowledged to numerous foreign diplomats that their Government has provided significant, direct financial support to the Government in Asmara.'

Dubai is also important as a centre from which the Eritrean government provides funding for its operations around the Horn of Africa. Hard currency is provided to the Eritrean embassy in Nairobi, from where payments have been made to armed groups operating in Somalia and elsewhere.

Significant as these Arab donors and hubs are, they are not the only sources of non-transparent funding for the Eritrean regime. There are at least three other income streams. These are the funds from the diaspora, who are forced to pay the Eritreans government two levies: a 2 per cent tax and a further tax to support the defence budget. Both of these will be dealt with in the chapter on the diaspora, but it is worth noting at this stage that according to the International Monetary Fund more than a third of Eritrea's funding comes from the diaspora, if one includes the remittances sent to family members. This was the IMF's conclusion in 2004: 'Diaspora are the largest single source of foreign currency inflows into the country, with the ratio of these transfers to GDP averaging 37 per cent over the last ten years.' This assessment came with a warning: 'These levels of diaspora financing are clearly exceptional; but even lower levels are achievable only if confidence and trust in government policies and economic developments are maintained and contracts are honored. Both fiscal and external sustainability depend critically on the continued support of the diaspora.' Sadly it is just this trust and confidence that is now lacking. On the plus side (for the government) it must be remembered that in the last decade mining has come on stream and it is possible that this percentage has fallen significantly.

The third source of hard currency is the trade in contraband goods and smuggling. Much of this is undertaken through Sudan, with General Teklai Kifle 'Manjus' controlling the Eritrean side of the border. He is reported to deal in electronic goods, sugar and alcohol, which are imported from the United Arab Emirates and sold to Sudan via a wealthy Khartoum businessman. Millions of dollars are also made from the sale of Eritrean scrap metal. In addition to this is the human trafficking outlined in the chapter on refugees, also controlled by General Manjus. Exactly how much is derived from these sources is—of course—a matter of speculation, but is said to be extensive.

* * *

The Eritrean economy is bifurcated. On the one hand there is the overt economy, with most citizens involved in peasant agriculture or the service sector (mainly government employment) and one major mine. On the other hand there is the covert economy, with its dodgy levies, taxes, donations and informal or illegal deals. This funds a good deal of President Isaias's foreign policy adventures: his attempts to undermine the Ethiopian regime by financing militias in Somalia and Ethiopia. It also provides Eritrea with the hard currency it requires to buy weapons and ammunition. These two economies—one hidden and one open—exist alongside each other. That both are real and functioning is well known to Eritrean citizens and—via the UN Monitors—the international community, even if the details are obscure. Little has been done by the UN to attempt to eradicate the non-transparent transactions, since this would require confronting the Arab regimes in the region—something neither the West nor the Russians or Chinese are keen to do.

8

THE FLIGHT FROM ERITREA

It is one of the saddest commentaries on the current situation in Eritrea that so many of its people flee the country. According to the UN Refugee Agency—the UNHCR—by the end of 2015 just over 475,000 Eritreans were refugees—or, as the agency puts it officially—the 'population of concern'. This represents around 7 per cent of the possible population.

Why is it that so many, mostly young people, are seeking refuge in another country?

It is by no means an easy choice. They have to make their way past borders guarded by troops with orders to shoot to kill. There is then the danger and uncertainty of life in exile: whether it is running the risk of being seized by people traffickers and held for ransom; dying in the wastes of the Sahara; or drowning in the Mediterranean. If they survive this they land up in a strange country, far from friends and family and begin to build a new life. It is hardly a tempting prospect, yet hundreds of thousands have chosen this path.

Given the gross human rights abuses and the lack of freedom it would not be surprising if some Eritreans opted for this risky choice, but this would not explain the vast numbers that flee the country—statistics that make Eritrea one of the highest refugee contributing countries to the European Union and the highest from Africa. To understand why Eritrean youth abandon their country it is necessary to outline the system of National Service, or conscription, since this is the main cause of the flight.

National Service

In its report, 'Just Deserters: Why indefinite national service in Eritrea has created a generation of refugees', published in December 2015, Amnesty International provided a useful summary of how conscription operates:

> In 1995, the Eritrean government issued the Proclamation of National Service (No. 82/1995) under which National Service, which encompasses active national service and reserve military service, was declared mandatory for men and women between the ages of 18 and 50. Active National Service is compulsory for all citizens between the ages of 18 and 40, followed by reserve duties. The initial period of service is meant to be 18 months, consisting of six months' military service followed by 12 months' deployment in military or government service.

> The objectives of National Service include, inter alia, "the establishment of a strong Defence Force based on the people to ensure a free and sovereign Eritrea; to create a new generation characterised by love of work, discipline, ready to participate and serve in the reconstruction of the nation; to develop and enforce the economy of the nation by investing in development work our people as a potential wealth; to develop professional capacity and physical fitness by giving regular military training and continuous practice to participants in Training Centers."

> The Ministry of Defence is responsible for National Service. In practice, other ministries are involved in the assignment of people to National Service positions which fall under the mandate. The National Service Proclamation also lays out the punishments for evasion or desertion, including for attempting to do either by trying to leave the country.

THE FLIGHT FROM ERITREA

In 2002, the government launched the 'Warsai Yikealo Development Campaign' (WYDC) where National Service conscripts were deployed to posts in the civil service, national and local administrations and state-owned companies, in addition to the military. The WYDC also extended the statutory 18 month period of service indefinitely.

The government cites aggression and the threat of invasion from its neighbour Ethiopia as the key justification for the necessity of indefinite service. After the two countries returned to armed conflict from 1998–2000, an independent Eritrea-Ethiopia Boundary Commission ruled, in 2002, in favour of Eritrea over a disputed piece of land occupied by Ethiopia. The ruling has not been implemented and the international community has made little effort to enforce the decision. Partly as a result of this, the government considers the country must be on a permanent war footing.

The rather cool language that Amnesty International uses is useful, but it does not quite capture the issues that people confront. In reality they are held in a form of permanent limbo. There is no fixed duration for conscription; it is indefinite. Some conscripts have been in National Service for twenty years and more. Although the Eritrean government has, from time to time, suggested that this will end, there is no evidence that this has been implemented. Most young people in National Service are paid a pittance. Exact figures vary but most sources agree that soldiers earn a monthly salary of about 500 Nakfa ($33) after completing their training and much less (less than 100 Nakfa per month) during the training. They face an impoverished, desolate life, bereft of hope.

For women there is an added danger: brutal sexual exploitation by army officers. The UN Commission on Human Rights in its lengthy report collected many testimonies of what took place. This is just a small selection of what the Commissioners were told:

A former trainer at Sawa military training centre told the Commission that the sexual abuse of young women in Sawa military training camp was 'normal.'

The Commission also heard from former conscripts that suggested the this practice is pervasive. 'Over 70 per cent of the girls were violated like that. Students are not allowed to go to the officers' rooms, but sometimes the officers ask them to come to their house. The girls cannot say no because they know what will happen in training if they say no. When they enter the room, the officers tell them to take off their clothes and they abuse them. The girls do not report it.'

Another former conscript reported: '90 per cent of the girls are destroyed. Girls don't even dream about a better life in Eritrea.'

The results of these abuses are predictable. Women are raped, fall pregnant, are humiliated and often rejected by their families and their communities. The UN Commission concludes that this behaviour is 'widespread and notorious' and that officers use their control over the recruits in a manner that 'amounts to torture' and 'sexual slavery.'

Confronted with indefinite conscription enforced by torture and sexual exploitation it is hardly surprising then that so many Eritreans will do almost anything to leave the country. This story is perhaps typical. It describes the case of a young man—given the name Abdu—not his real name. Like many young Eritreans he passed through Sawa, the country's main training camp. It comes from a series of 52 in-depth interviews conducted by the London-based Overseas Development Institute.

Abdu is from Asmara. He tried to stay in school for as long as possible to avoid entering Sa'wa—the education and military camp all Eritrean youngsters are forced to join. To no avail—by the time he was 20, in 2007, Abdu had to join. The camp was located in a volcanic area called Wia, with high temperatures (48–50C) and no grass, no trees. Young people died because of the heat; others lost their mind. There were two basic meals a day (bread and tea in the afternoon and bread and lentils for tea).

After six months he was moved to a different camp and asked to work as a cameraman for the state channel. He had no say in the matter, yet he was relatively lucky. Others had to work in construction, moving stones and building dams for 16 hours a day for the equivalent of £7 a month. He saw no future there, even though he was doing better than others.

His first attempt at escaping was in 2008. He was caught at the border and jailed for two years and seven months, until 2010. In jail, he was made to dig holes every day; he doesn't know why. Abdu was released five months earlier than his original sentence dictated, and was told by officials, 'We give you mercy.' Abdu disagrees: 'But it's not mercy. They took two years.'

After he was released, Abdu was sent back to his previous work place. Finally, he could contact his family again. He now knew that if he tried and failed a second time to escape, he would be killed, not jailed. So he stopped thinking and continued working.

In February 2014, he got permission to visit family in Asmara. During that time, the Ministry of Defence discovered there were some missing tapes in the archives Abdu was handling. Abdu's colleague was asked where the tapes were, but he didn't know so was taken to prison. One of Abdu's friends called him and warned him. After calling around and talking to an uncle, Abdu decided to escape and moved towards the Sudan border.

So desperate have some National Service conscripts become that they will seize almost any opportunity to escape. On Sunday 3 April 2016 vehicles carrying conscripts were driving through Asmara, on the way to the port of Assab. Reports of what took place are sketchy, but what appears to have happened is this. Two conscripts decided to take their chance as they passed through the city and jumped from the truck. They were immediately shot dead by guards. But the conscripts had alerted their families and a city bus was used to block the road. When the vehicles halted, other conscripts made a run for it. The guards, determined to halt the escape at any cost, opened fire, shooting into the crowd. A total of twenty-nine people were killed or injured. Six died on the spot and eighteen were taken to Halibet hospital.

For five days the government said nothing, but because the names of the injured were published on opposition websites the authorities were forced to admit that there had indeed been an incident. Two died and eleven were injured 'when they jumped and fell from military trucks,' tweeted Yemane Gebremeskel, the government spokesman. 'Police stablilized z situation by firing few warning shots into z air.' [sic] Why the troops risked their lives by jumping from the trucks and why shots had to be fired to 'stabilise the situation' was not explained.

Official collaboration in trafficking

How is it that so many thousands manage to cross the border, when it is patrolled by the military, whose troops have orders to shoot to kill?

Part of the answer is that the frontier lies in remote, rugged terrain, which is difficult to patrol. But there is also evidence that officials, including some of the highest military officers, are involved. Although there were rumours that this had taken place for some time, the first evidence came in 2011 from the UN Monitors. Their report pointed to General Teklai Kifle 'Manjus', commander of the Eritrean border forces as well as the western military zone, as being at the heart of this operation.

The Monitors laid out in considerable detail the role General Manjus played in smuggling arms across the border (in violation of the UN sanctions regime) as well as his links with senior Sudanese officials. The experts then explained the general's role in human trafficking:

> The well-documented exodus of young Eritreans to escape poverty or obligatory 'national service' represents yet another opportunity for corruption and illicit revenue. People smuggling is so pervasive that it could not be possible without the complicity of Government and party officials, especially military officers working in the western border

zone, which is headed by General Teklai Kifle 'Manjus'. Multiple sources have described to the Monitoring Group how Eritrean officials collaborate with ethnic Rashaida smugglers to move their human cargo through the Sudan into Egypt and beyond. This is in most respects the same network involved in smuggling weapons through to Sinai and into Gaza.

According to former Eritrean military officials and international human rights activists, military officers involved in the practice charge roughly $3,000 a head for each person exiting Eritrea. Eritreans seeking to leave the country illegally (i.e. without an exit visa), and who can afford to pay these fees, often choose to do so rather than risk imprisonment.

In some cases, however, smugglers may demand an additional ransom payment up to $20,000 per head in order to release their charges. An Eritrean directly involved in smuggling operations into Egypt explained to the Monitoring Group how family members are required to send the funds via money transfer agencies to Eritrean officials operating in the Eritrean embassy in Egypt, and in Israel, in order to secure the release of their relatives.

Although the Government of Eritrea prohibits human smuggling, and has reportedly imprisoned some officials for taking part in it, senior Government and/or party officials linked to General Kifle's command profit from the practice. The Monitoring Group has obtained details of a Swiss bank account into which the proceeds from smuggling have been deposited and has provided the Swiss authorities with information related to this account, together with the personal and contact details of the Swiss-based coordinator of this trafficking ring and details of the co-ordinator's Egypt-based associates.

The report also described the smuggling network from Eritrea to the Sinai that was organised by two officers under General Manjus's command. An informant told the UN Monitors that the officers received next to nothing for their work: 'Manjus gets all the money. They don't get anything. They are in the military so they just do what they are told.' The 2011 report was referred to and supplemented in subsequent years.

Survivors of human trafficking interviewed by Professor Mirjam van Reisen, Meron Estefanos and Conny Rijken described how the Border Surveillance Unit drove them out of Eritrea. They were hidden under covers in trucks and four-wheel drive vehicles so as to avoid border check-points. Members of the Eritrean diaspora in Western countries paid $5,000 to $7,000 for a safe passage to get a relative out of Eritrea. This meant that: 'you pay a high rank official, the relative doesn't get checked at the checkpoints, the official will drive your family member all the way to Khartoum and that is where he receives the money.'

Other researchers have corroborated their conclusion. A report by the Sahan Foundation and the IGAD Security Sector Program described how Eritreans with sufficient money and connections pay for a comfortable four-wheel vehicle to take them to Khartoum and are simply put on a flight to a European capital:

> Not all migrants and refugees are obliged to face the hazards of desert and maritime journeys described above: some smugglers offer 'first class' treatment—at a price. These include a number of well connected Eritrean smugglers operating from Khartoum, who conduct complex international smuggling operations, organising flight connections to remote international destinations, from where European visas are obtained for their 'passengers'. Chief among them is an Eritrean individual known as 'John Habtu' (aka 'Obama'), who allegedly holds citizenship in the Netherlands, but who owns a property in Leeds, and who for a price of $20,000 or more per head is organising travel of people from Sudan to Singapore and the Philippines, from where his clients are issued European visas and flight tickets to Europe. During the last week of August 2015, the Singaporean authorities made some arrests of Eritreans at Changi airport, which may have been connected to 'Obama's' smuggling operations.

> Another Khartoum-based smuggler using the Singapore route is known as Awet Kidane. One Eritrean migrant paid Kidane $30,000 to travel from Khartoum to Belgium via Singapore. Once in Belgium, the travel-

ler's family members were instructed to transfer money to contacts in Sweden and Dubai, a system of payment similar to that employed for land-based travel through Libya.

The Sinai route

The route via the Sinai resulted in some of the worst abuses inflicted in recent years. Once crossing into Sudan Eritrean refugees contacted traffickers who were meant to guide them across the Red Sea and then into Israel. Instead many were sold to local tribesmen. The lengthy report by van Reisen, Estefanos and Rijken provided graphic detail of how Eritreans were treated by the Bedouin. Held in the most appalling conditions—often little more than holes in the earth—the Eritreans were given phones and told to contact relatives anywhere in the world. They had to extract thousands, sometimes tens of thousands of dollars, from their relatives and friends to win their freedom. The captives would be tortured, abused and raped—while on the phone. One technique that was frequently used was for a plastic bag to be set on fire and for the burning material to be dropped onto the flesh of the victim as they spoke to family members across the world: in Dubai, London, or Asmara. The screams of agony persuaded the relative to raise almost any sum the traffickers demanded. While working for the BBC I interviewed one victim while the torture was taking place: one of the most harrowing experiences of my career as a journalist.

There were also reports of organs—including kidneys—being taken from some of the victims. So pervasive was this practice, and so disgusted were ordinary Eritreans, that they are reported to have daubed graffiti on houses in Asmara. 'You built this house with the kidneys of our children,' declared one sign painted on the home of two colonels.

For those women who became pregnant the outlook was horrifying. This was one victim's testimony.

UNDERSTANDING ERITREA

I was still in chains when I gave birth. In fact I was tortured in the morning, and in the afternoon my labour came and I gave birth in the evening. I tore off my clothes to cover the baby... There was this other woman who gave birth three months earlier, and there was another lady who was held with us, they helped me. She asked them to get us a blade to cut the umbilical cord, and they brought her a corrugated rusted piece of metal and she had to use that one... They didn't give me anything.

It is not possible to arrive at a conclusive figure for the numbers of Eritreans, Sudanese and Ethiopians who were subjected to these abuses. The researchers estimated that one of the gangs involved in this trafficking between 2009 and 2013 handled 15,000–20,000 people. And the mortality rate was high—between 5,000 and 10,000 did not survive.

The Sinai route is now closed: Israel constructed a barrier to further entry. A fence, six to ten metres high, now snakes along the Israeli border with Egypt in the Sinai. Costing $524 million, the security fence has resulted in a dramatic reduction in the number of Africans entering Israel. In 2012–2013 over 10,000 arrived, but this figure fell to just 200 in 2015.

The Libyan route

By 2016 Libya was the main route that Eritreans used to try to reach Europe. Once they crossed into Sudan they moved to the capital, Khartoum before using a people trafficker to reach the Libyan coast. Every step had to be carefully planned, generally using mobile phones. Relatives, friends and fellow countrymen advised on the most appropriate route, but none was safe. Many were held in a transit camp near Khartoum known to migrants as 'Hajar', or as 'Kilo 105'. Situated in the arid lands north of Khartoum the camp served as a final staging point before smugglers moved the travellers into Libya. All along the way were hazards: trucks that broke down, traffickers that demanded additional payments, attacks from bandits. Many did not make it. Images of bodies and bones littering the Sahara are not difficult to find on the internet.

There are also reports that the torture camps, pioneered in the Sinai, are being replicated in the ungoverned spaces of Libya. There is currently an additional threat, this time from so-called 'Islamic State' or ISIS. Meron Estefanos, a Swedish-Eritrean who monitors the plight of refugees closely, said that in mid 2016 as many as 1,000 Eritreans were being held by ISIS in Libya. She believed that the same group had killed at least 100 Eritreans between February 2015 and May 2016. Her research indicated that at least 200 Eritrean women were among those who had been taken captive: sixty to seventy have managed to escape. The women were forced to convert to Islam (if they were Christian) and then given away as 'brides' or slaves. An ISIS fighter was allowed to choose as many as he wanted—depending on his seniority. It was only once they had been given as 'gifts' that some managed to escape. Before that they were held captive in closely guarded compounds. Over forty Eritrean women who were held captive by ISIS have managed to escape and arrive in Europe, providing Meron with first-hand testimonies of what they had endured.

Despite the dangers involved, Libya remains an important escape route for Eritreans, but this is something the EU is determined to halt. An embryonic Libyan government now operates from Tripoli and despite the evidence of abuse, EU officials are working with the new authority to intercept the refugees at sea by the Libyan Coast Guard. On 20 June 2016, the EU extended its anti-smuggling naval operation in the central Mediterranean to include training the Libyan Coast Guards and Navy, which are intercepting boats and sending migrants and asylum seekers back to Libya. The EU is also asking NATO to assist its operation.

'The EU isn't sending people back to Libya, knowing that's unlawful, so it wants to outsource the dirty work to Libyan forces,' said Judith Sunderland, Associate Europe and Central Asia Director at Human Rights Watch. The operation is being strengthened by a European naval force, operating from a base in Rome. Sandro Gozi, Italy's European Affairs Minister, revealed the plan in an interview with the BBC. He explained in May 2016 that the EU naval force will 'soon' be able to 'stop the trafficking in Libyan territorial seas.'

Since October 2015 there has been UN authorisation for naval forces to intercept boats in international waters. UN Security Council resolution 2240 allowed for international navies to 'inspect' and 'seize' vessels involved in human trafficking—but only on the high seas. The UN approved action inside Libyan coastal waters, but only in the context of cooperating with the Libyan Government. When this resolution was passed no such government was in place. But in March 2016 a 'National Salvation' government backed by the UN arrived in Tripoli. The new government operates from within a heavily guarded naval base, but this has not prevented the international community from recognising it. With its permission the EU and NATO now operate inside Libyan territorial waters. This allows navies to destroy the boats and other facilities operated by the people smugglers without putting at risk any refugees or migrants who are already at sea.

The British government has already deployed a warship to the area. All that is needed is a formal request from the Libyan government for the operation to begin.

David Cameron told the G7 summit in Japan in May 2016 of his plans. He argued that it was a global challenge that required a comprehensive solution, and reiterated his desire to work with the Libyan government to help them build the capacity of their coastguard. The aim would be to help them 'intercept boats off the coast, both those carrying migrants and those carrying arms'.

'We will now take an active leadership role in that process. Four military planners have deployed to Rome this week to the HQ of Operation Sophia, the naval mission in the Mediterranean, where they will work with other EU colleagues to agree a plan going forward for the Libyan coastguard,' Mr Cameron said. 'Once that is established we will then send a training team to assist the Libyan authorities in improving their coastguard maritime operations. Then, once the relevant UN security resolutions are in place, we intend to deploy a navy warship to the region to assist in the interception of arms and human smuggling.'

The Libyan route out of Africa appears to be closing—a trend that can be seen from Morocco in the West to Israel in the East. 'The EU—soon perhaps with NATO's help—is basically deputizing Libyan forces to help seal Europe's border,' commented Judith Sunderland, of Human Rights Watch. As Libya became increasingly dangerous Egypt has emerged as one of the few remaining alternatives. But travelling to Italy by Egypt is longer, more costly and even more dangerous than the journey via Libya. Until recently Eritreans who were arrested by the Egyptian authorities were deported to Ethiopia, but since mid-2015 this route has been blocked. Some are now forcibly returned to Eritrea—even if they were registered with the UNHCR as refugees when they were in Sudan.

Smuggling networks

These hazards have not dissuaded Eritreans from making the journey. A total of 157,000 Africans crossed from Libya to Italy in 2015, with Eritreans making up the largest percentage of this total, at just over 39,000. FRONTEX, the EU border agency, has an interesting take on the Eritreans who make this journey. This is from a press release issued on 18 February 2016. They concluded that the difficult and complex journey relied on a well-organised system:

> the route from Eritrea seems to be controlled by one sophisticated network managing the whole journey, starting from Eritrea going

through Sudan, and then into Libya. This means that the payment is made to the same network, usually using the Hawala system—an informal way of transferring funds based on honour code operating outside traditional financial channels.

Just who runs this 'sophisticated network'? A publication by the Sahan foundation and IGAD (the Horn of Africa regional grouping) in February 2016 provides some useful answers. Their work is based on investigations by the Italian authorities who began following the tragedies near Lampedusa in October 2013 and September 2014, during which some 800 migrants and refugees drowned. The investigations, 'Operation Tokhla' and 'Operation Glauco 2', uncovered a good deal of information about the smuggling networks. Importantly, they revealed the key ringleaders in these networks:

> The Tokhla investigation resulted in several arrests, including Maesho Tesfamariam, one of the Eritrean ringleaders responsible for organising the ill-fated journey of September 2014 and who, at the time of his arrest, was based in Germany. Authorities also arrested 24 people in Sicily as a result of the Glauco 2 investigations in June 2015, most of whom were Eritrean nationals.

> Glauco 2 exposed the modus operandi of two other prominent smugglers formerly based in Libya: Medhanie Yehdego Mered (born in Eritrea), and Ermias Ghermay (born in Ethiopia). The two men are portrayed by Italian prosecutors as the most prominent individuals responsible for coordinating the transfer of human cargoes through Sudan and Libya. Ghermay, who has operated from the notorious beachhead of Zuwara near Tripoli, is known to have been responsible for organising the vessel that sank off the coast of Lampedusa in October 2013.

> The investigation demonstrates his communications from his base in Zuwara with collaborators in Sudan, Sweden, Switzerland, as well as calls to Israel in relation to financial payments. Since the investigations concluded, numerous credible sources in Libya have reported that Ghermay has gone to ground and may no longer be a major figure in the world of human smuggling in Libya.

THE FLIGHT FROM ERITREA

These smuggling operations flourish in the lawlessness that has gripped Libya since the overthrow of Colonel Gaddafi in October 2011. Eritreans are, of course, not the only ones to use this route. The South Africa-based think-tank the Institute for Security Studies reports that since 2013 around 100 trucks a week have been leaving Niger, each carrying twenty-five to thirty-five migrants from West Africa, all heading to Libya.

After the drownings off Lampedusa the EU sent naval forces to try to prevent a repeat of the tragedy. This had unforeseen consequences. The Institute for Security Studies reports that instead of taking their human cargo all the 160 nautical miles to Italy, the smugglers now have the goal of taking them just twelve nautical miles: into international waters. At this point—say survivors—they are transferred from fishing vessels into large rubber dinghies. One of the migrants is given a satellite phone and a number to call—usually the Italian Coastguard. This is, as far as the smugglers are concerned, the end of their responsibility. If the migrants are lucky the naval vessels find them, and transport them to Italy. The warships have become taxis for the traffickers, only rarely arresting anyone involved in this trade.

The smuggling operation is extremely lucrative. These are the sums calculated by the Institute for Security Studies:

> Payments to armed groups or local militia in order to have a secure departure point make up a large proportion of the costs incurred by smugglers operating through Libya. Other expenditures include bribes of up to US$100 at each land checkpoint while transporting migrants by truck; up to US$5,000 a month for renting a 'safe house' where migrants are kept under surveillance while they await departure; up to US$80,000 for a boat that will hold 250 migrants; around US$4,000 for a rubber dinghy to ferry groups of 20 migrants to a waiting vessel; US$5,000–7,000 paid to a captain to pilot the larger craft out to international waters; and roughly US$800 to buy a satellite telephone for migrants to call for rescue in international waters. These costs are easily covered by the revenues

generated by charging groups of 200 migrants, with each paying between US$1,000 and US$2,000, depending on circumstances.

The smugglers can therefore charge up to $400,000 for each crossing, from which the costs itemised above must be deducted. The authors calculate that similar smuggling operations through Egypt can net the traffickers as much as $60,000 per crossing.

The Ethiopian route

So far the discussion has revolved around the flight into Sudan, and from there into the Sinai, Libya or Egypt. But another major route exists—south into Ethiopia. Over the years tens of thousands of Eritreans have chosen this means of leaving their country. It is no easy journey. This is the conclusion of the North Africa Mixed Migration Task Force, consisting of a range of humanitarian organisations:

> Eritreans cross the border to Ethiopia by foot and often at night to avoid detection because of the risk of being shot or detained by Eritrean border guards. All interviewees reported being very scared when fleeing Eritrea. Some of them crossed in groups of up to eight people, some with just one other person and some on their own. The crossings took place in rural areas away from main roads, but the areas where the interviewees had crossed where close to Rama, Gerehu Srnay, Zalambessa and Badme on the Ethiopian side. All of them had been found by Ethiopian soldiers who had taken them to the closest police station. From there they had been sent to the main registration centre for Eritrean refugees in Endabaguna and later to one of the four refugee camps located in the Tigray region.

By December 2015 the UN Refugee Agency (UNHCR) estimated that 131,000 Eritreans were living in Ethiopia. The majority are housed in camps in Afar and Shire, in Tigray region in Northern Ethiopia. Others are in the barren Afar region.

These camps are seldom visited by the international community and even less frequently reported in the media. Mai Aini camp in Tigray is hardly an inviting destination. A journalist who visited in 2014 for the Israeli paper, *Haaretz*, provided this vivid description of what conditions were like.

> We drove along a dusty, unpaved road to get to the place, stuck at one of the hottest, lowest points in northern Ethiopia, near the border with its neighbor and former enemy Eritrea. The refugees descend from the highlands of their home country, fleeing from the torture, forced conscription and labor, religious persecution and other human-rights abuses of their authoritarian government, to cross the border from Eritrea into Ethiopia and, accommodated by Ethiopia's 'open door' policy, they are immediately placed in the camps.
>
> Unless they are among the lucky few with a family in Ethiopia to sponsor them, it is unlikely that a new refugee family will leave the camp any time soon. There, they may languish for years, under the watchful eyes of armed soldiers manning checkpoints to ensure their confinement.
>
> As we neared the camps, signs of the people['s] desperation became evident; the surrounding areas were nearly barren as a consequence of the refugees' ceaseless hunt for wood to fuel their cooking fires. Once inside the first camp we visited, Mai-Aini, the air felt hotter and denser, and it was thick with dust. There was no running water.
>
> With the assistance of outside agencies, why do conditions in the camps remain so dismal? 'It is very complicated,' said Dr. Bereket Berhane, an Eritrean refugee living in Addis Ababa and chairman of the Eritrean Youth Global Movement, who was our guide for this visit. 'Ethiopia is a poor East African country. I'm thankful for what they are doing. The refugees are being hosted in a safe area where they have water and firewood. There are tens of thousands of refugees, and the indigenous community itself is struggling from day to day. There is only so much a country can do.'

Life in the camps is crushingly boring; there is little to do and all the time in the world to do it. Many of the refugees are children, what the aid agencies term 'unaccompanied minors'. Rudimentary education is available, but little more. There are art classes, during which the children can paint about their experiences and their fears of the fate that lies ahead of them. For some the prospect of living in a desolate camp with no hope of a better future is too much to bear. They leave, crossing into Sudan in an attempt to find a way of reaching Europe—no matter how risky that might be. This is the experience of an Eritrean interviewed by the North Africa Mixed Migration Task Force:

> All refugees in the camp know the problems on the road to Libya. But because of the small chances for resettlement everybody will try to go the illegal way. At this time of the year the weather is good, so maybe I will go after one month. I fear it a lot, but because I have no other option I have to go. There are lots of people I know that have gone. Some of my friends have made it to Europe and others have died.

To deal with this issue the Ethiopian government introduced a policy of allowing Eritreans to live 'out of camp.' Since 2010 they can be granted permission to live in Addis Ababa or one of Ethiopia's other cities. The government has also begun to allow some of the refugees to study at university, but they remained no more than a small minority.

Addis is estimated to be home to some 8,000 Eritrean refugees. For some this has been vital—deterring them from attempting the dangerous sea route to Europe. 'Previously I had plans to take dangerous journey to reach Europe via Sudan and Libyan Desert; but I dropped my decision after I was granted a work-permit that would allow me to be out of camp,' Baraki explained. He is now employed at a workshop where he earns money to support himself. 'I would rather stay here in Ethiopia until the repressive regime [back home] is overthrown and a democratic government replaces it,' he said. One of his friends drowned while trying to reach Italy via the Mediterranean in 2015.

THE FLIGHT FROM ERITREA

The long road

The journeys that Eritreans make to seek a better future are extraordinarily difficult and dangerous. A study by the Overseas Development Institute in London found that some arrived at their final destination in just two and a half months; others took up to seven years. All along the way obstacles had to be negotiated. Sometimes journeys were broken for years at a time as Eritreans were held captive, or had to work their passage. One couple who were interviewed worked in Libya for just over a year, with the man on construction sites and his wife employed as a maid, before moving on to Europe. The study found that it cost most Eritreans an average of £3280 to use the Mediterranean route via Libya and Italy:

Biniam, 28 years old, paid £2,540 for a year-long journey. This was his path.

- Sawa, Eritrea: At the age of 12 he was rounded up and taken to Sawa camp, for national service. For the next 15 years he was based at Sawa, only being allowed to visit his family in Asmara when his superiors let him.
- Tesenay, Eritrea: In 2013, at the limits of his endurance, he decided to leave. He moved to Teseney, close to the Sudanese border, where he worked on the farm of a relative. Unsure whether to move on, Biniam sought the advice of a friend on the farm. 'We had built a trust. He told me to go for it.'
- Khartoum, Sudan: A few days later, Biniam was in Khartoum.
- Benghazi, Libya. Sudan wouldn't be a safe place for a defected Eritrean to stay. So using savings, Biniam paid smugglers to get him to Europe via Libya. The trip cost around £2,000 and time in prison.
- Sicily, Italy (2014): From Zuwarah port, it took Biniam four attempts to cross the Mediterranean. He finally made it in October 2014 when a passing ship rescued them and took them to Sicily. Before he could be fingerprinted by authorities, Biniam made a dash for Milan.

- Calais, France (2015) Unimpressed with Milan, Biniam continued onto the UK. After a three week wait in the Calais 'jungle', trying every night to creep into vehicles, Biniam finally made it across the Channel by hiding in a truck's cargo.
- Bolton, UK (2015) He was eventually allocated accommodation in Bolton, and in June 2015 granted asylum by the British government.

Biniam's journey is one among many and each is different. Some involve even more complex and circuitous trips via South Africa, Latin America and the Caribbean to reach their chosen destinations. An Eritrean who landed up in Cape Town explained that he had been waiting ten years for South African immigration officials to decide on his status, which was still designated 'asylum pending.' His most viable route to a more secure life was to pay smugglers to go through South and Central America to the United States, but the costs are prohibitive—as much as $30,000.

* * *

As one route closes another will be investigated and then used, but remaining in their own country is, for many Eritreans, simply not an option. The brutal repression and the prospect of an indefinite existence as a National Service conscript convinces many that they should head for the border. The journey they face is littered with obstacles. Only the richest can afford to bribe their way onto a Land Rover to Khartoum, or onto a flight leaving Asmara. Officials and human traffickers take their cut and even then there is no guarantee of safe passage. The emergence of ISIS or Islamic State has only compounded the hazards. Yet thousands of young men and women make the decision to flee from the country that they know and love.

9

EXILE

LIFE FOR THE DIASPORA

For the hundreds of thousands of Eritreans who have left their country the hazardous journey into exile is only the beginning of their ordeal. Memories of life at home come flooding back: of walking the streets of Asmara; sipping coffee in a café; sharing good times with friends. The peace of Eritrean villages; the bleating of goats; the children all around. Even the smells and tastes of home seem irresistible.

Exactly how many Eritreans live abroad no one knows. As with so many aspects of Eritrean life the facts are clouded and obscure. Until Independence in 1993 many were classified as Ethiopians. In 1994 the UN Children's Fund, UNICEF, estimated that one million Eritreans had fled their country, which amounted to nearly one out of every three Eritreans—if the total population was correctly estimated. This figure was also used by the World Bank in its study of Eritrea at the time of independence: 'Of an officially estimated population of about 3 to 3.5 million, as many as one million Eritreans were forced to leave the country due to the repressive policies of the military regime.' The diaspora is to be found in almost every corner of the globe: from Australia to the United States; from South Africa to Norway. Few have chosen to go home since independence, but very few have forgotten their homeland. This is the dilemma of Eritrean exile.

Early exiles

As Professor Gaim Kibreab, the foremost scholar on the Eritrean refugee experience, points out, the decision to flee the country began with the war of liberation in 1961. Conflict with the Ethiopian government drove many to seek sanctuary in Sudan. From there they gradually re-built their lives and moved on to other countries. Many remain in Sudan: 117,320 were known to the UN Refugee Agency in January 2015.

Sizeable communities live across the region, in Egypt, the UAE and Bahrain as well as Europe, North America and Australia. They have put down roots, established families and got on with their lives. They are to be found in every walk of life—from cleaners and taxi drivers to social workers and lawyers. As with many diasporic communities, they have often done better than the native populations through hard work and perseverance. But no one should underestimate the sacrifices they have made and the suffering of individuals—some of whom have been deeply traumatised by the escape route they took as well as the isolation, racism and indifference they experienced in their host countries. To counter this Eritreans did what other exiles had done before them: they started restaurants in which they congregated; they established societies, churches and mosques that reflected their faiths and inclinations. In other words, they formed communities.

From the first the liberation movements worked hard to retain their ties with the diaspora. Indeed, the EPLF was reliant on the diaspora for its very survival. As Professor Kibreab explains, the movement established a range of bodies to tie them to its struggle, since the Front had few other sources of finance:

In the early 1970s, three Eritrean diaspora organisations emerged in the Middle East, Europe and North America. These were the Eritrean General Students' Union (GUES), Eritreans for Liberation in North America (EFLNA) and Eritreans for Liberation in Europe (EFLE). Even though the GUES maintained a veneer of autonomy, it was from the outset affiliated to the ELF. Although the EFLNA and the EFLE mobilised massive material and political support for the EPLF, in the beginning, they were not formally affiliated to the Front. This was not because of the EPLF leadership's respect for autonomy of civil diasporic organisations, but rather to shield them from the influence of its Foreign Mission, which was until March 1976, headed by the energetic Osman Saleh Sabbe. Osman Saleh Sabbe was in favour of affiliation of the diaspora organisations to the EPLF, but the field leadership preferred to see that the EFLNA and EFLE maintained a thin cover of temporary formal autonomy.

In March 1976, the EPLF leadership accused the head of its Foreign Mission, Osman Saleh Sabbe, of conspiring behind its back to form a united Front with the ELF and after an acrimonious confrontation severed its relations completely. Sabbe withheld all financial and logistical assistance in an attempt to pressurise the leadership of the EPLF to submission. When the flow of external resources dried up suddenly, the EPLF leadership made a U-turn and appealed to the leaderships of EFLNA and EFLE to be affiliated to the Front and to substantially increase their financial contributions.

The response from the exiles was extraordinary: few other diasporic groups could match their commitment. Across North America and Europe EPLF supporters abandoned their studies and took up full time work in order to fund the movement. They moved into crowded apartments to save money so that they could increase their donations. There are even tales of some eating pet-food in order to reduce their expenditure. The North American organisation raised over $200,000 from around 500 members—an average annual contribution of $400. The European branch, with 3,000–4,000 members, many of them living in Italy, contributed between 10 and 20 per cent of their meagre incomes. Students gave from their grants or scholarships; European branches organised street collections.

These commitments bound the exiles tightly to the liberation movement. In this case their loyalty was to the EPLF, but other political organisations, including the ELF, benefitted from similar generosity down the years. For those enduring the lonely years of exile it was a way of re-asserting their Eritrean identity. Whenever their country has been really challenged the response has been the same: they rallied to the cause. Yet although the movement they supported was heavily reliant on external funding this did not result in the diaspora having a real say in the policies of the EPLF. Under Isaias control always remained tightly centralised; the exiles might advise, but they did not exercise much influence. In this sense the EPLF was very different from South Africa's African National Congress. The ANC leadership was outside the country during the liberation struggle and it was from Lusaka or Dar es Salaam that they attempted to guide the movements that were active inside the country. The EPLF was based in, and remained inside, Eritrea.

The identification with the country that the exiles felt did not evaporate at independence. When the border war erupted in May 1998 much the same level of external support was to be seen. Victoria Bernal, at the University of California, recorded what took place:

> In June 1998, for example, Eritreans met in Copenhagen and pledged $1,000 per household; in Riyadh they pledged one month's salary each; in Edmonton, Canada $26,000 was raised on the spot at a single meeting. Jubilant reports of these and other meetings circulated via the Internet on the U.S.-based Eritrean website, www.dehai.org. A message reporting on a meeting held in St. Louis on June 14 where $55,000 was pledged in two hours stated, 'St. Louis resident Eritreans made history and a lesson to share with other brothers and sisters. This is something that all Eritreans need to emulate.'...

In response to these efforts, the Eritrean government promptly set up a national defense bank account and the donations flowed in. It is worth noting, moreover, that these donations were not earmarked as humanitarian aid to alleviate the suffering caused by war but were aimed at bolstering the Eritrean state's capacity to wage war. Tekie Beyene, governor of the Bank of Eritrea, described the contributions from the diaspora as 'beyond anybody's imagination.'

These contributions were made at a moment of severe crisis. Eritrea's continued existence appeared to be at stake as Ethiopian forces drove deep into the new state's territory. The diaspora was glad to play its part and the contributions were, in the main, entirely voluntary. During the border war exiled communities purchased Eritrean bonds worth $36.5 million and made contributions of $106.4 million. The total contribution to the war effort reached $142.9 million. As we shall see, this generosity was exploited and the willingness to pay was gradually eroded.

Financial payments were not the only means by which Eritreans were bound to their state. During the war of liberation the EPLF cleverly came up with the idea of organising a giant festival in Bologna. First held in 1974, it attracted thousands of Eritreans from across Europe. They came together to share their culture, network and raise money for the movement. Improvised hotels, bars and cafes were established and hundreds of thousands of dollars were raised for the struggle. The festival was a chance for exiles to let their hair down, to eat, drink and socialise with other Eritreans. It was a very popular event. Smaller scale festivals were developed in other European locations, as well as becoming a feature of life in North America.

In Germany there were similar commemorations. Martyrs' Day, on 20 June, was a particular moment for the community to gather in public. In Frankfurt, for example, trees were planted and candles lit to commemorate the dead. Gatherings were held in virtually every German town with an Eritrean community. In a park in

Nuremberg there is even a memorial dedicated to the martyrs of the Eritrean revolution. It consists of a plaque, mounted on a low brick pedestal, and a tree behind it. A stylized olive wreath is engraved on the plaque and below it an inscription in German and Tigrinya reads: 'This tree was planted in memory of the people who gave their lives for Eritrea's independence. We will never forget them—The Eritreans living in Nuremberg'.

As the reality of life back home became clear support for the festivals and commemorations gradually ebbed away. Criticism of the regime increased as the word spread of the wave of arrests in September 2001 that saw leading critics of the president and independent journalists rounded up. As exiles realised that their anticipated state, based on human rights and the rule of law, was receding into the distance, they began to lose faith in the Eritrean government. Attendance waned and contributions fell. Although no one forgot the sacrifices made to achieve their country's independence, some chose to recall the dead in the privacy of their own homes, rather than at government sponsored events.

This is not to suggest that the Eritrean government and President Isaias are without genuine supporters, both inside and outside the country. But their numbers have been in decline. If it was not for the continued stalemate with Ethiopia, and the lack of action by the international community to enforce the Algiers Agreement that ended the border war, opposition might have spilled onto the streets. Professor Gaim Kibreab quotes a telling interview he conducted in 2003 with an elderly chairman of one of Eritrea's regional assemblies. After turning off his tape-recorder, the interviewee said:

Look, I am almost 70 years old, and I do not fear anything for my life, but as long as danger is shadowing our nation and as long as our enemies are still on our necks, my conscience will not allow me to oppose and demonstrate. This is a nation built by blood and sweat of my children. We need our unity more than ever, when now, again, the international community has betrayed us. The moment the border is demarcated and our sovereignty is safeguarded, I will be the first to go out in the street and demonstrate.

As Professor Gaim suggests, the old man probably spoke for many of his generation.

From willing contributors to coerced exiles

Today Eritreans living abroad face a range of pressures, planned and organised by the regime. These have two aims: to increase the revenues received by Asmara and to keep the Eritrean diaspora quiescent and supportive. It has left many fearful for their families back home and isolated from their communities abroad.

One of the most important means of extracting this revenue is via what became known as the 2 per cent tax. Officially the 'Rehabilitation Tax' it was imposed under Proclamation 17 of 1991 and Proclamation 1 of 1995. These stipulated that: 'Every individual with a salary pays 2 per cent of a rehabilitation tax from gross monthly income.' It applied to citizens wherever they lived—inside the country or abroad. The penalty for non-payment is severe: denial of all assistance from the Eritrean government. No embassy will provide support and no official is allowed to deal with anyone in the diaspora if this payment has not been made.

These are some of the measures that this ruling applies to: obtaining or renewing an Eritrean passport; obtaining an Eritrean ID card or other crucial records including marriage, death and birth certificates; the purchase, sale or inheritance and transfer of property throughout Eritrea; obtaining land for house construction in one's village of origin; sending consumer goods, such as sugar, clothing, edible oil, wheat flour, etc. to one's family; claiming unaccompanied luggage on arrival in Eritrea. Before any of these measures can be undertaken proof must be provided that the 2 per cent tax has been paid in full. Students are required to contribute at a lower rate, but everyone is required to pay—and the payments are backdated to the moment that employment began.

Since 2011 the international community, as represented by the United Nations, has attempted to prohibit the 2 per cent tax. Security Council resolution 2023 condemned its collection, which—the resolution said—was used to 'destabilize the Horn of Africa region' and for purposes including 'procuring arms and related materiel for transfer to armed opposition groups or providing any services or financial transfers provided directly or indirectly to such groups.' The Security Council called for action saying that it: 'Decides that Eritrea shall cease using extortion, threats of violence, fraud and other illicit means to collect taxes outside of Eritrea from its nationals or other individuals of Eritrean descent.' All states were asked to halt the collection of the tax.

The resolution was passed after strong statements from Somalia, Djibouti and Ethiopia. The Ethiopian prime minister, Meles Zenawi, accused Eritrea of violating the security of the region and went on to present a long list of complaints. He said that Eritrea had:

> invaded islands held by Yemen before it had invaded Ethiopia. It had also invaded Djibouti, first denying it had done so, and then admitting it had by withdrawing and allowing Qatari troops to replace its own. Further, it had publicly stated it would arm and train any group willing to remove the regime in Khartoum. It had characterized the regime in Somalia as a puppet regime and was arming Al-Shabaab to further destabilize that country.

Prime Minister Meles concluded with these words: 'The problem was not a lack of communication, but one of attitude, resulting from a certain clique in Asmara that had never grown up from a rebel group. It was also a problem of lawlessness.'

The Eritrean government appears to have decided not to participate in the debate and there was little support for the Eritrean position from any African state; both Nigeria and South Africa attacked what the Eritrean government had done. Other representatives were equally critical. Speaking for the United Kingdom, the ambassador, Mark Lyall Grant, 'expressed concern about Eritrea's disruptive activities in Somalia and the region' and 'urged Eritrea to comply with this and all other Council resolutions.'

Given the overwhelming support for the resolution one might have assumed that it would have been enthusiastically enforced, but this has not been the case. Britain, despite having called for compliance, has done little to ensure that the tax is not being collected.

US and Canada crack down

Eritrea has been in trouble with North American governments for several years. In the 1990s Eritrea's Washington embassy had established a money-transmitting business in the American federal capital. In August 2000 this was taken over by a company, Himbol Financial Services. This provided a transfer system for American Eritreans, as well as the country's nationals in other parts of the world. In 2001 Himbol hired Kesetbrhan M. Keleta to run the business, which he did for the next year. Although Kesetbrhan attempted to obtain a licence for this operation his application remained pending. Despite this he continued to send the remittances—around $10 million in total—until he left Himbol's employment at the end of 2002. He was found guilty of running the business without a licence and sentenced to thirty-one months in jail. Kesetbrhan appealed to the Supreme Court, but his petition was denied.

In 2009 the US State Department ordered Eritrea to close its consulate in Oakland, California, charging the Eritreans with using remittances to fund Somali rebels of al-Shabaab. The Bush administration gave the Eritreans just ninety days to shut the mission, complaining about Eritrea's behaviour in Somalia and interference with the activities of the American embassy in Asmara. In a briefing for reporters, Jendayi Frazer, Assistant Secretary of State for African Affairs, said US officials believe that taxes on the earnings of the estimated 200,000 Eritreans living in the United States, collected by the Oakland consulate, had been used to finance weapons and training for Somali insurgents. Frazer said tensions with Eritrea that pre-dated the Bush administration had been escalating, with Asmara refusing to grant visas to American officials assigned to the US embassy in the capital and demanding to inspect diplomatic pouches. Whether the American action succeeded in halting the 2 per cent tax is a moot point. It is more likely that it was transferred via another route.

When the Canadian authorities discovered that the 2 per cent tax was being extracted from their nationals, they acted. In 2011 newspapers reported that the Consulate General of Eritrea in Toronto was behaving as a fundraising front that solicited a 2 per cent income tax and a $300 to $500 'national defence' fee from the Eritrean diaspora. In May 2013—after investigating the allegations—the government expelled the Eritrean Consul. The Consul, Semere Ghebremariam O. Micael was told to leave Canada for persistently violating the UN sanctions regime. Canada's Minister of Foreign Affairs, John Baird, said Mr Micael had been declared persona non grata and gave him a week to leave. 'Canada has repeatedly made clear to Eritrea to respect international sanctions and Canadian law,' the Department of Foreign Affairs said in a statement.

Even this did not end Eritrean activities. A year later there were further newspaper reports that the 2 per cent tax was still being extracted. In May 2014, as a condition for maintaining a diplomatic post in Toronto, Eritrea agreed that the consulate would not have any role in the solicitation and collection of taxes. But several Eritreans who phoned the Toronto consulate said they were still being instructed to pay the tax. They tape-recorded the conversations as evidence the consulate was still an active player in the taxation scheme. At this point the Canadian authorities appeared to have given up, ending their campaign to halt the tax collection.

British enforcement of the tax ban

The British government assured the UN that it took steps as early as 2011 to ensure that the diaspora tax was not being collected in the UK. This was referred to in the 2012 report by the UN Monitoring Group:

> On 20 May 2011, the Government of the United Kingdom notified the Eritrean authorities that, since aspects of the collection of the two per cent tax may be unlawful and in breach of the Vienna Convention on Diplomatic Relations, until it was demonstrated otherwise, the Eritrean embassy should suspend, immediately and in full, all activities relating to the collection of the tax.

The Foreign Office said it had reminded Eritrea that the diaspora tax was illegal. In a parliamentary answer Baroness Warsi explained that: 'On 20 December 2012, Foreign and Commonwealth Office officials raised these concerns with the Eritrean ambassador and reminded him of UN SCR 2023.'

Despite these assurances and repeated warnings, it is clear that the British government's policy has been continually flouted by the Eritrean embassy. The British government is fully aware that this has taken place. In its report to the UN Security Council in July 2013, the UN Monitoring Group had this to say about the diaspora tax: 'the Group has obtained receipts, dated 2012 and 2013, which document taxation by the Government of Eritrea of its citizens living in the United Kingdom, Italy, Sweden and Canada, and it has been reliably informed by dozens of Eritrean citizens living in the diaspora of taxes being levied in other countries with significant Eritrean populations.'

To strengthen the British resolve, Eritreans living in the UK decided they would provide the government with evidence of the pressure they were under. Simon Tesfamariam, who has dual British and Eritrean citizenship, went to the Eritrean embassy on the morning of 18 December 2013. He went as an ordinary Eritrean to get official clearance to allow him to do business in the country. Unlike other Eritreans he was wearing a secret camera during the visit.

This is a transcript of his conversation with Eritrean Embassy staff:

> EE: What was your address when you last paid?
>
> ST: When I paid? 90 Guinness Court I think. [his previous address]
>
> EE: Since then, there hasn't been any payment.
>
> ST: Well it's probably because I was still a student then. I was told to pay for my ID card.
>
> EE: Yes, you paid for ID card. You were underage so 2% tax was not applicable. Bring your ID.
>
> ST: From when do I need to pay according to this?
>
> EE: OK... The year you were born is 1978, right?
>
> ST: Yes.

The Embassy staff member then consults with another member of staff before returning to Simon.

> EE: In 1996, you turned 18 years old. You have not paid anything since 1996. If you were a student, you have to bring proof of that.
>
> ST: Well I was a student until 2001, until I finished university.
>
> EE: You have to bring proof if you were in college or university.
>
> ST: So I have to bring proof that I finished university?
>
> EE: OK, you know you were under age until 1996 and then from then until 2001, in education. Proof is needed or if you were under social services and so on.
>
> ST: Well, I was under social services from 1995 to 1997 but not after that. I was living in a children's home.

EE: OK from 1996 to 2004 what were you doing? Were you working, studying, you have to bring proof. Anyway even if you were a student, £50 per year is paid by everyone. For the rest, until 2013 you have to provide proof of income.

Before 1996, you don't need to. However, after and until 2013 you need to bring a payslip, a P60 or anything that indicates your income. When you come with all these documents, then you can pay the 2% tax.

ST: Do I have to pay it all at once?

EE: No you don't have to pay it all at once; you can break it down and pay in Eritrea.

ST: So do I have to pay it in Eritrea?

EE: Yes you have to pay it in Eritrea.

ST: But do I have to go myself? How can I?

EE: You can send it.

ST: OK, so it has to be paid there in pounds?

EE: Yes in pounds. However if you have anything to do and there is any query, for example Power of Attorney, or anything to do there, you will have to pay it all and get clearance. You will not be able to do anything without clearance. However, if you have no query or nothing to do, then you can pay it little by little.

ST: But I don't get clearance until everything is clear.

EE: Yes, clear.

Simon Tesfamariam's experience is common. Every Eritrean resident abroad must pay the 2 per cent tax before their embassy is permitted to provide any assistance to the individual. But—as the transcript makes clear—instead of collecting the money in the UK and transferring it to Eritrea, the embassy instructs their citizens to make the payment directly to Eritrea. This has allowed the Eritrean authorities to claim that they are not collecting the tax at the embassy. It is clearly a ruse, since the outcome is identical.

This evidence was presented to the British Foreign Office, but to little effect. The Eritrean government continued to demand payments, which the Eritrean embassy ensures are sent to Asmara.

In 2013, under pressure from the diaspora, the British government met the Eritrean ambassador, as well as members of the Eritrean community. This was revealed in a parliamentary reply on 24 February 2014 by Baroness Warsi:

> The UK supports United Nations Security Council resolution (UNSCR) 2023, which condemned Eritrea's use of the Diaspora tax and called on Eritrea to cease using illicit means to collect the tax. The UK has made clear that the use of coercion or other illicit means to collect the tax in the UK must cease. Foreign and Commonwealth Office (FCO) officials last raised this on 25 October 2013 in a meeting with the Eritrean Ambassador. On 8 November 2013, officials from the FCO, the National Crime Agency and West Yorkshire Police met members of the Eritrean Diaspora to discuss the Diaspora tax. At this meeting, Eritreans were urged to report any use of coercion or other illicit means to collect the tax to the police. We will continue to engage with the Diaspora on this issue.

The implication was clear: the British authorities regarded the tax as 'illicit' (rather than illegal) and that coercion to collect it had to end. But the United Kingdom was not about to launch any investigation of its own; rather it was calling on Eritrean exiles to complain to the police if they were being forced to make a payment. This was a somewhat unusual way of enforcing a UN Security Council resolution—especially one that the British government supported. Nonetheless, British Eritreans set about collecting evidence to present to the police.

In March 2015 a group of Eritreans went to a central London police station with the evidence. 'We wish to register a criminal complaint against the Ambassador of the Embassy of Eritrea, 96 White Lion Street, London N1 9PF, as advised by the Foreign and Commonwealth Office,' they said in an accompanying letter. They continued: 'A colleague, and a fellow member of the Eritrean community living in the UK, Temesghen Debessay Asfha, was required to pay a tax to the Eritrean government in order to wind up his affairs in Eritrea. On 26 May 2014 he was told to pay the tax of £350 in Eritrea and was instructed that if this was not paid in full his affairs would not be concluded. This included a charge of £200 for the Eritrean military.' They presented evidence in the form of receipts. They went on to declare that the tax collection is 'a clear violation of the assurance given by the Ambassador to the Foreign Office on 25 October 2013 that the tax collection had ended.' Explaining that the tax was being extracted from one of the poorest communities in Britain, they asked for the expulsion of the Eritrean ambassador. Having obtained a receipt from the police, they left, hoping that action would follow.

On 15 April 2015 Chief Inspector Claire Clark wrote to the complainants acknowledging that their report had been made. Ms Clark said she had asked her Parliamentary and Diplomatic Protection Department to investigate the allegations. In the end the evidence was not considered sufficiently strong to bring a prosecution and no further action was taken.

Western governments appear to have given up attempting to halt tax collection in their countries by the Eritrean government. Although it is clear that considerable coercion is being exerted through Eritrean embassies no effective action is being pursued by the U.S., Canada, Britain or any other nation—despite their nominal support for the UN sanctions programme.

Israel deports 'infiltrators'

Chapter 8, 'The Flight from Eritrea', outlined the route to Israel via the Sinai. For many years Israel was seen as an important potential place of refuge. Before the construction of the giant security fence mentioned above, many thousands of Eritrean refugees made the journey. There are now around 43,000 African migrants in Israel, mostly from Eritrea (some 31,500) and Sudan (around 8,500).

The Israeli government is a signatory to the United Nations refugee convention, but almost no one is ever granted full refugee status. Israel has one of the lowest rates of refugee registration in the world: 0.16 per cent of applications are successful. This is not surprising: they are not classified as refugees, or even as migrants, but as 'infiltrators'—a term the Israelis devised to deal with Palestinians attempting to return from exile. Ethiopians Jews who come to Israel (who call themselves 'Beta Israel', rather than 'Falasha', which is considered derogatory) are regarded very differently. As Jews Israel considers they have a 'right to return' and are therefore treated as citizens, even though they sometimes face discrimination. In 2010 there were 110,000 Israelis of Ethiopian extraction.

According to three campaigning organisations, the Aid Organization for Refugees and Asylum Seekers in Israel (ASSAF), Amnesty International and the Hotline for Migrant Workers, Israel deals with its African refugees under a policy of 'temporary collective protection.' The groups explain what this means in practice:

> By utilizing this policy, the government of Israel acknowledges the danger in these... countries and does not deport asylum seekers to their countries of origin. Asylum seekers are given deferred deportation orders, which render their stay in Israel legal. This documentation, however, does not allow them access to formal work permits, health care or welfare services. Asylum seekers are stuck in a legal limbo; while being allowed to remain in the country, they lack access to basic services in order to survive, advance, and integrate.

Israel's Eritrean community therefore lives in a twilight world: unable to integrate, but not deported. Many have been rounded up. Israel has two detention centres to which they are sent. One is a 'closed detention centre' or prison, called 'Saharonim'. Others are held in a smaller detention centre, 'Holot', which is designed to hold around 3,300 prisoners. Most are single men arbitrarily picked from the refugee community. Some have been in the country for several years. 'Holot' is in a remote desert location, fifty kilometres from the nearest town. The detainees are under constant pressure to leave the country voluntarily.

They face the option of remaining in indefinite detention, or accepting a passage to a third country. Some have taken the second option. According to Israel's Population, Immigration and Border Authority, 2,920 asylum seekers accepted deportation in the first eleven months of 2015. But this was fewer than half the number of asylum seekers who left in the same period the previous year. The Aid Organization for Refugees and Asylum Seekers says that the Israeli government has not provided information on how many returned to Eritrea. Nor have they been able to find out what happened to anyone who accepted this option. 'Human rights organizations have not managed to establish contact with any asylum seekers who left Israel in order to "voluntarily" return to Eritrea over the past two years. Despite all efforts, it is unclear how many of them returned to their homeland and what became of them.'

Eritreans who have been 'willingly' put on planes have been sent to Rwanda and Uganda. On leaving Ben Gurion International Airport they are given Israeli travel documents, but on arrival in Uganda or Rwanda these are—by all accounts—removed from them. They are provided with cash, but this is soon used up. They are required to check into a local hotel, which charges $100 to $150 a night—normally the sum for a month's stay. From then on they are on their own. They are in Rwanda or Uganda illegally, subject to arrest and deportation to their country of origin. This, despite the Israeli Supreme Court ruling that human rights are grossly abused in Eritrea. The Eritreans are, effectively, in yet another double bind: in a strange country, without papers. There are also reports that they are monitored and threatened by agents of the Eritrean government if they engage in critical journalism or speak out against the regime.

The Aid Organization for Refugees and Asylum Seekers report concludes:

> Asylum seekers coming to Uganda can contact the Ugandan Prime Minister's Office, charged with caring for asylum seekers, to request refugee status and receive a three-month residency permit, serving also as an identifying document. However, reports indicate that it is hard to complete this process without entry permits to Uganda. None of those interviewed for the present report managed to complete the process, although some have been in the country for about a year. The asylum seekers reported economic hardships, and most of them testified that they still did not feel safe in Uganda. Leaving Uganda presents difficulties as well. One of the interviewees explained that leaving Uganda is not always possible: 'Someone tried to cross the border to South Sudan and they took all of his things, his clothes, and sent him back to Kampala. Six friends went to the border. They took their suitcases and put them in prison for 15 days. Three were told to go back, three moved to South Sudan.'

The situation in Rwanda is similar. Eritreans find themselves without papers, fearful and no further forward in their search for a safe home.'

Why do Uganda and Rwanda accept Eritreans (and Sudanese) deportees from the Israelis? In 2013 the Israeli paper *Haaretz* published a lengthy report in which a number of human rights groups alleged that both African countries were being provided with Israeli arms as a reward for taking the 'infiltrators'. The governments deny that there is a 'refugees for arms' deal. Rwanda's Foreign Minister Louise Mushikiwabo is quoted as saying: 'Israel is a good friend of Rwanda and we work together closely, especially in the fields of agriculture and technology, but there is "no special package" for the refugee question.' The Ugandan authorities also said that they were unaware of any deal. The Israeli prime minister's office, when asked about the programme said: 'The Israeli government led by Benjamin Netanyahu has completely halted the illegal infiltration into Israel and is determined to continue returning to their countries of origin the thousands of illegal migrant workers who have entered here. All actions are taken in accordance with international law.'

Whether or not an arms deal is part of the package for Uganda and Rwanda it is clear that Eritreans are under intense pressure to leave Israel. As Human Rights Watch concluded in 2014:

> Israel's policy of facilitating the departure of Eritreans and Sudanese to third countries, such as Ethiopia, Rwanda and Uganda, also puts it at risk of violating its international obligations. Without legally binding formalized transfer agreements with these countries including assurances that they will have access to full and fair asylum procedures, there is a risk that Eritreans and Sudanese transferred to these countries could also be victims of refoulement.

Spooks, threats and internet trolls

It is one of the burdens that Eritrean exiles have to bear that even when they have escaped from the repression that has engulfed their own country they are not free. When I participated in a public meeting at the University of London in 2014 with Dan Connell, I experienced some measure of the pressure that is exerted on the opposition abroad. We were heckled and an attempt was made to shout us down. The youth wing of the ruling party— the YPFDJ—are among the most actively involved in these attempts at intimidation. We had to call in the University security to allow the talk to proceed. An Eritrean government website described Dan Connell and me as being an 'Axis of Evil'. Eritreans in exile are treated much more ruthlessly.

A network of spies and informers has been carefully nurtured by the Eritrean regime to monitor and control their citizens abroad. The Eritrean diaspora is under constant surveillance— and they know it. Go to almost any Eritrean opposition gathering and you will see them: young men and women who gather information and intelligence on anyone who steps out of line. Anyone who challenges the regime cannot go home for funerals, weddings or other family events. The doors of their homeland are firmly closed to them.

On the other hand it is important not to underestimate just how powerful the psychological hold of the regime is over its diaspora. Many were brought up by their families to identify strongly with the movement and its leaders. A good number still hold these views. It requires a real wrench to break with these ties. For some it leads to isolation from their own parents, for whom the EPLF had an almost mythical status.

Sometimes this involves violence. When members of the opposition attempted to protest during the 2014 Eritrean government festival in Bologna they were attacked by pro-government security staff. In the first incident, two members of the official security staff attacked demonstrators, injuring two of them. One needed stitches in his head, the other to his head and back. The festival security staff were identified by the distinctive T-shirts they wore, with 'Eri blood' written on them and a picture of a red heart. The following day—when opposition continued—a government supporter drove a car into the demonstrations. Again a member of the opposition was injured and needed medical treatment.

Much of the government's effort is more subtle, but no less intimidating. There are accusations of Eritrean agents hacking into computers and mobile phones belonging to members of the opposition, while members of their families are harassed and arrested inside the country. The UN Commission of Inquiry found a range of examples of this kind of intimidation. They uncovered spies that operate around the world—a sophisticated network that keeps the diaspora under constant surveillance.

Some of these examples involve the collection of the 2 per cent tax. One witness who reported having been a spy for an Eritrean embassy told the Commission that:

In 1997, Mr. [A], the consul in [a foreign country]... called me for a meeting joined by other spies. They told us we should continue our struggle in [a foreign country]. He introduced us to each other and started meeting us individually. There was an organisation... We were assigned to this organisation, not to work but to ensure the PFDJ was represented in every organisation. They wanted me to join the board. I refused, arguing I was too young and inexperienced. Later, Mr. A told me he had a job for me. He told me I should work for them as a security agent in [city Z]. He said this would only be between him and me.

Later, he gave me appointments and said I would always be able to enter the consulate, without needing permission and without having to wait for an appointment. Even the people at the consulate were not allowed to ask us any questions. I received a schedule for the entire week. I was asked to go every day to different hotels or restaurants. There were three shifts per day. We were asked to chat with people who came to those places and report on what we heard. Every day, I had to report back to the consul in person. I believed this was the right thing to do ... We had to observe every religious group. Those working in the religious groups are church members and PFDJ members at the same time... We did not know who was an agent and who was not. The work was organised by the consul alone, not with others. Now they have people who don't trust each other. At the time, it was different... I decided to discontinue my work with them.

Other forms of intimidation concern spying on Eritreans who are considered to be political dissidents or engaging in religious activities not authorised in Eritrea.

One witness explained to the Commission that: 'My brother and my father cannot go back to Eritrea because they belong to the opposition party. There are spies in [a foreign country] who spy on what Eritreans do there.' Another person told the Commission that: 'People cannot speak freely. Even here in [a foreign country], Eritreans cannot speak freely because the Government of Eritrea sends people to spy on those who have fled Eritrea.'

The Commission says that many of its witnesses spoke about the fear of returning to Eritrea to visit because they might have been blacklisted as a result of their political and other activities. Others explained that they felt constrained to join organisations in the diaspora or express free opinions regarding the situation in the country. 'Most importantly, the Commission found that there are legitimate fears among Eritreans in the diaspora that the Eritrean Government engages in phone tapping and email surveillance in Eritrea such that they cannot freely communicate with their relatives in the country.'

There was also evidence of the web of spies the Eritrean authorities use to intimidate the diaspora, using threats of retaliation of family members back home.

A witness told the Commission that:

> When I left the country, the security forces kept on asking my wife if I was coming back or not. They made frequent visits to the house. They tried to make her their informant so that they could extract information about my activities. They thought that I was involved in political activities. In 2008, due to the visits and harassment, she packed and left the country with the children.

The Commission quoted a further witness as saying that while he was living abroad, his mother was approached by national security officers: 'One day when going to work she spoke to a woman in the intelligence unit who said to her "Your son is very active in the opposition, why don't you tell him to just concentrate on his studies?" to which my mother replied "You know today's children, they don't listen to their mothers."'

The cumulative effect of this pressure has left its mark on the exile community. They are cautious and sometimes even fearful about expressing their opinions openly. There is a sense in which they are only partly separated from an abusive state, and still in awe of its ability to influence their lives.

There is, however, one group of exiles that is not affected by such pressures. They are the relatives of senior Eritrean government officials who continue to support the regime. A number have sent their families abroad in recent years; some for study, some to remain. So the family of General Sebhat Ephrem, former Minister of Defence and currently Minister of Mines and Energy, lives in Sweden. The daughter of General Filipos Woldeyohannes, Army Chief of Staff, has been living in Uganda. Quite why they have been sent abroad is unclear, but it may serve as a form of insurance against what the future might hold in store.

Using the courts

A quiet, but well-orchestrated, campaign has been underway in the Netherlands. The Eritrean government has attempted to use the Dutch courts to try to silence its critics. The cases were brought by leaders of the youth wing of Eritrea's ruling party— the Young People's Front for Democracy and Justice (YPFDJ), but the campaign is guided by senior government officials, including some close to President Isaias. No fewer than seven court cases were opened against liberal newspapers, a radio station, a website, the Dutch government and an academic: Professor Mirjam van Reisen.

The first to face the courts was Mirjam van Reisen, a professor of International Relations at the University of Tilburg. An adviser to the European Union and the UN, Professor van Reisen is a well-respected expert on Eritrea. In May 2015 a Dutch website, *Oneworld.nl*, published an article alleging that some of the interpreters working for the Dutch immigration service were linked to the Eritrean regime.

They were hired to translate sensitive conversations between officials and refugees who were seeking asylum. Many of their clients had fled from Eritrean state repression. For the translators to have links to the Eritrean government was contrary to the regulations governing the Dutch immigration service. These stated that: 'Neither you, nor your family in first or second degree are (or have been) involved with a regime with which foreigners claim to have experienced problems.'

When asked about these links Professor van Reisen described them as worrying. 'Many Eritrean asylum seekers are immensely traumatised,' she said. 'When the refugees discover that the interpreters are linked to the regime they fled from, this undermines their trust in protection by the Dutch authorities. In addition, it arouses fear. The interpreters get sensitive information about the asylum seekers through the interviews that they translate. With this information, they may threaten these refugees. Relatives inside Eritrea may also be threatened.' The article identified the brother and sister of the president of the Dutch youth wing of the ruling party (the YPFDJ) as being among the translators. 'The interpreters are linked to the centre of the (Eritrean) intelligence in the Netherlands and across Europe,' Professor van Reisen said.

On 23 May 2015 the president of the YPFDJ in the Netherlands, Meseret Bahlbi, went to a police station and filed a charge of libel and slander. He asked for an apology, correction and a fine of a minimum of €25,000. The case came to court on 10 February and—to the immense relief of Professor van Reisen—the accusation was rejected. Her right as an academic to freedom of speech was upheld. The judge found that the YPFDJ had indeed received instructions from the ruling party. Further the judge ruled that among the goals of the YPFDJ are to 'act as informants for (the embassies of) the regime in Eritrea'. Perhaps at least as damaging for the Eritrean government was an admission by Meseret Bahlbi that the regime engages in torture.

Although this case backfired, others were pursued. One was against the Dutch migration agency. Brought by Bahlbi's siblings the court once again found against them. There were also two cases against *Volkskrant*, the country's foremost liberal newspaper, but these were also lost. Despite this the complainants have not abandoned the cause and have appealed against several of the judgements.

The campaign has been accompanied by vociferous attacks on social media. Van Reisen has been physically threatened. Both she and I have been demonised, quite literally—with one Tweet portraying us as vampires, with blood dripping from our mouths. Some attacks are faintly amusing, but they have to be taken seriously since they are orchestrated by a government. In 2015 Yemane Gebreab, President Isaias's closest political adviser, told 550 young Eritreans attending the party's youth rally in Germany that fighting the country's 'enemies' was their top priority. 'We have to remember, always remember, that we have still enemies who plot on a daily basis,' Yemane told the conference. 'Enemies who don't tire and don't sleep, who try to bring our downfall... Therefore, our first objective—as YPFDJ and as Eritrean youth, and as community... the objective which still remains at the very top of the list, is to conclusively defeat this hostility hovering over of our nation. That remains the job.' In this context of the network of Eritrean government agents operating around the world the Dutch campaign takes on a new, and more sinister, significance.

These issues were grasped by the Dutch Parliament in June 2016. Its MPs passed a resolution calling for strict measures to halt the infiltration of the immigration service by YPFDJ cadres together with a string of restrictions on Eritrean government supporters. There was also a demand for conditions to be attached to EU aid for Eritrea.

* * *

There has been a gradual transformation in the position of Eritrea's exile community. Numbering several million and spread across the globe, some have consciously turned their back on their past and concentrated on forging their lives in their new homes. But most have maintained close ties with their country of origin. In the 1970s and 1980s some went to extraordinary lengths to support the war of independence. The achievement of that goal in 1993 was given an ecstatic welcome, but as the reality of the new state emerged their enthusiasm gradually waned. When President Isaias turned on his colleagues and arrested them in 2001 it sent a shock wave through the diaspora. Some continued their support, but over time dissent gradually grew. What had been pride and joy turned to resentment and finally to determined opposition.

Today there is a deep split between backers and opponents of the Eritrean government. There is one not very obvious source of strength for the president: the willingness of key individuals to continue to work with him and support his administration even though members of their own families have been brutally mistreated. Seyoum Tsehaye, the head of the country's radio and television service, has been jailed without trial since September 2001. Yet his brother, Alem Tsehaye, continues to serve as Eritrean ambassador to India. The ambassador to Kenya, Beyene Russom, is the husband of a well-known prisoner of conscience, Senayit Debesay. The Eritrean ambassador to France's sister, Ruth Simon, who worked as a journalist for the French news agency, AFP, was only released from jail after many years of imprisonment. The Swedish-Eritrean journalist, Dawit Isaak, perhaps the country's best-known political prisoner, is in a similar position. His brother, Tedros Isaak, who also lives in Sweden, is a staunch supporter of the regime.

President Isaias has sent his lieutenants abroad to bolster support among the exiles. At first this took the form of persuasion and encouragement, through festivals and meetings. As these gradually proved ineffective more drastic measures were introduced. Today Eritreans abroad are under intense pressure to pay taxes to Asmara and to provide the regime with uncritical backing. Anyone who steps out of line can expect to come under intense pressure. This takes the form of social pressure and blocking access to their families back home. In parts of Africa this can be far more severe. Eritrean security forces operate in Sudan and South Sudan and are capable of attacking or kidnapping dissidents. Exiles in Uganda complain that they are threatened, abused and sometimes assaulted.

Some in the diaspora have decided to keep a low profile, but others have refused to be cowed and have attended mass rallies against the regime from Washington to Geneva. It is striking that in June 2016, when the Commission of Inquiry report was being debated by the UN Human Rights Commission, refugees in Israel clubbed together to hire a fleet of twenty-two buses to bring protesters from the Holot detention centre in the Negev desert to make their views known in central Tel Aviv. Even in the most difficult of circumstances members of the diaspora are now determined to oppose the regime.

10

OPPOSITION

The Eritrean government's control over its population is pervasive, oppressive and totalitarian. The regime attempts to ensure that nothing escapes its purview. Internally its network of spies and informants is said to have extended to recruiting children who make their living by selling cigarettes and sweets on the streets. Abroad the regime's activities are equally vigilant, as described above. Yet despite this, opposition to President Isaias is growing—and, most worrying for the president, it now reaches the streets of Asmara. Political resistance takes two forms—internal and external—and I will consider each in turn.

Internal resistance

Soon after the liberation of Asmara in 1991 the first signs of disquiet became evident. Women fighters complained of their treatment; the disabled called on President Isaias to address their needs; and the veterans took to the streets demanding that they be paid. All were ignored and their concerns dismissed. Their leaders were arrested and jailed. Instead of meeting their grievances they were treated as little more than traitors for questioning the president and the party that he led. Reasoned criticism was snuffed out. A climate of intolerance was established that has become increasingly stifling as the years have gone by.

These developments came to a head during and after the border war with Ethiopia. They culminated in the confrontation with the G15—who had been some of the president's closest and most loyal supporters. They were arrested in 2001, together with all independent journalists. A government sponsored mis-information campaign was unleashed against them. This was organised by *bado seleste* (literally Zero Three). Former ambassador Andebrhan Weldegiorgis has described Zero Three as a 'presidential disinformation service' used to discredit Isaias's opponents.

Dating back to the liberation struggle, it was used to spread rumour and gossip against anyone thought to oppose the ruling party. This rumour-mill was used to attack the G15 prior to their arrest, portraying them as 'un-patriotic' and 'traitors.' Following the arrests of the G15 internal opposition went quiet. People grumbled in private, but there was little outward expression of dissent.

Yet the government's portrayal of Eritrea as a peaceful, contented nation is clearly wide of the mark. Several attempts have been made against the president's life. In August 2009, for example, troops tried to kill him on the road between Asmara and the port city of Massawa. The assassin was named as Lieutenant Daniel Habte Yihdego, who is said to have opened fire on the president's car, before exchanging fire with his body-guards. The presidential car was damaged, but Isaias escaped unharmed. He was said to have been severely shaken by the attack. The president reverted to the practice he adopted during the liberation struggle of changing his sleeping arrangements and travel plans at the last moment, to prevent a repetition of the attempt on his life. However, nothing was done to address the underlying discontent.

Isaias made elaborate plans to ensure his security. This was the assessment of the American ambassador to Eritrea, Ronald K. McMullen, in a cable dated 18 February 2010, provided via Wikileaks:

> To protect himself and his regime from assassination, coup d'etat, army mutiny, or a foreign commando strike, Isaias has created three separate Presidential Guard units of about 2,000 troops each, according to a well-connected Eritrean businessman. These elite solders get extra pay, have modern equipment, and receive specialized training. Most are currently stationed in or near Asmara, including a sizeable group lodged about 800 yards from the DCM's (Deputy Chief of Mission) residence. The three units are nominally led by Major General Filipos, but in reality Isaias personally commands each one. In addition, Presidential Guardsmen also serve as jailors for the G-15 (senior Eritrean officials arrested in 2001). Isaias' right-hand man is Colonel Tesfaldat Habteselassie, who commands the 70-man presidential bodyguard detachment.

Operation Forto

On the morning of 21 February 2013 tanks rolled into Asmara for the first time since the Ethiopian forces had been driven from the city in 1991. The events that unfolded represented the most significant internal challenge Isaias had ever faced. No definitive account of the revolt has been written and what follows has been pieced together from various sources.

In the early hours of the Monday morning troops from the Tserona area, close to the Ethiopian border, converged on the town of Dekemhare, some 40 km south-east of the capital. They arrived in the town with twelve tanks, needing fuel. When the local garrison refused to provide it they seized it. The soldiers then headed north, arriving on the outskirts of Asmara at around 10:00 a.m. They sent three tanks to secure the airport, with the rest entering the city about fifteen minutes later, to the astonishment of the residents. The mutineers had assumed that other units from the rest of the country would join them, but they failed to materialise. Was the revolt betrayed, or did other officers get cold feet? There is no clear explanation, but for the rebels who were now inside their capital the die was cast.

The first major objective was the Ministry of Information building on a small hill overlooking Asmara. Known as 'Forto' it is home to the state broadcasting station, Eri-TV. Around 100 troops surrounded the building and gathered the staff into one room. The head of Eri-TV, Asmelash Abrha, was marched into the studio and forced to read a communiqué the mutineers had prepared. This called for the implementation of the 1997 Constitution and the release of all political prisoners and those caught fleeing the country. But after just a couple of sentences the TV station went off the air—officials loyal to the president had managed to cut the signal.

This was not how the mutineers had planned it. They had been tipped off that the president himself would be at the information ministry, continuing a meeting with regional administrators. But—in line with his security practices—the venue had been changed at the last moment. President Isaias was in his office. At this point there was something of an impasse. The president was safe; the rebels in control of the ministry.

Isaias sent the commander of the mechanised brigade, Colonel Tsehaye Mekonen, to negotiate with them. The rebels were led by Colonel Sied Ali Hjay (better known as Wedi Ali) who was the hero of the defence of the port of Assab against the Ethiopians in 2000. A confrontation ensued during which Colonel Tsehaye was shot and wounded. Wedi Ali is said to have ordered his tanks to open fire on the President's Office. They hesitated—reluctant to shell their own capital. Two of the most senior military commanders loyal to the president (Brigadier General Eyob and General Sebhat Ephrem) then appealed to the troops. The generals declared that they shared the rebels' aims. They begged them, in the name of the martyrs, to end the rebellion and to present their grievances to the government. Discussions went on into the early hours of the evening, with promises being made that the soldiers would not be arrested. No agreement could be arrived at and the rebellion started to unravel. Fearing that they would be captured, some of the rebel officers left the city, only to be surrounded and taken prisoner. Wedi Ali managed to evade capture for a while, but when he was finally tracked down he defended himself before committing suicide.

The rebellion was over and Isaias had survived. So why had it failed? Firstly, because the plan had gone off at half-cock, with their supporters in other parts of the military failing to join them. They may also have been betrayed, which would explain the last-minute change of venue for the president's meeting. Secondly, military radio communications were apparently under the control of the President's Office, leaving the rebels no other means of contacting the rest of the army. Finally, men like General Sebhat had remained loyal, even though he was reputed to be critical of the slow pace of democratisation. He had refused to sign the G15 letter to the president in 2001 and although he had been sidelined he was not prepared to join the revolt.

The diaspora followed every twist and turn of this story via every news-source they could find. Some went further. Protesters entered the Eritrean embassy in London in support of the rebellion and there were similar scenes in Stockholm, Frankfurt, Rome and Houston. For a moment—just a moment—there was hope among the opponents of the regime that their day had finally come.

The government later attempted to dismiss the events as a 'small incident'. Thomas Mountain, an American journalist sympathetic to the government, described the revolt as a 'tempest in a teapot.' It was three weeks before Isaias went on television to give his version of events. 'A handful of people stormed the building of the Information Ministry,' he said. 'We were surprised.' The president claimed that the troops who joined the rebellion had been 'brought to Forto by deception and under false pretexts' and when divisions emerged 'many of the soldiers abandoned the conspirators and left Forto.' By the following day the rebels had, 'whether voluntarily or forced, come forward and repented saying they were deceived and asked for forgiveness.' Wedi Ali was encircled and committed suicide. 'This brought the film to its end,' the president declared. The rebellion had been defeated but opposition was not at an end.

Revolt in the diaspora

There was a time when Eritreans in exile who were critical of the regime were quiescent. Many still are, fearful of the consequences for their families back home. Others genuinely believe in what the president and his government are doing. But an increasing number now challenge the regime.

Since November 2011 a group of dissidents have been attempting to find new ways of challenging President Isaias. The group, calling themselves 'Freedom Friday' (or 'Arbi Harnet' in Tigrinya), hit upon a plan of contacting Eritreans by phone to ask them to stay at home on a Friday evening, rather than going out on the town. Meron Estafanos, a human rights activist who had worked for years to help save Eritreans drowning in the Mediterranean, was the public face of the movement. 'We believe in a non-violent solution,' she said. 'We can't ask the people back home to go out and be killed. So we reversed the Arab Spring and appealed to people to stay in their homes.' Using automated phone calls, they contacted Eritreans. Making up to 10,000 calls an evening Freedom Friday asked people to remember the religiously persecuted one week, and those who died another.

OPPOSITION

On 18 September 2013 the Freedom Friday Movement launched an underground newspaper, twelve years to the day after the government closed all privately owned newspapers and arrested their journalists. Called 'MeqaleH Forto' or 'Echoes of Forto', it drew its inspiration from the failed rebellion. Distributed by supporters inside the country it carried articles in Tigrinya and Arabic describing the resistance movements inside and outside Eritrea. Soon copies were being read by the populace, or left in public places. These were followed by posters, pasted up in the dead of night, defying the regime. None of this is without risk for those inside the country. Some activists have been arrested and imprisoned, but still the campaign goes on.

Opposition parties and organisations

Once the Eritrean government could count on the unwavering support of the majority of the population inside the country as well as among the diaspora, but that is no longer the case. Internal resistance has, so far, been held at bay, but among the exiles there is growing confidence. Pro-government demonstrations are now met with competing demonstrations by the opposition. 'It is a question of contesting the political space,' was how one opposition supporter put it. Whenever there is a major event, whether it is the annual Bologna festival, or the launch in Geneva of the UN Commission of Inquiry report on Human Rights, both sides call on their supporters to make their views known. On occasions these have led to direct clashes. Both camps mobilise their activists and thousands converge on the chosen location. It would be untrue to suggest that either side has the upper hand. The balance of forces swings between pro-government members of the diaspora and critics of the regime, but the days of unequivocal support for the regime are over.

There are a plethora of organisations that oppose the current regime, all of which originated from the Eritrean Liberation

Movement of the late 1950s. Perhaps as many as fifty are in existence, although many are defunct and some have less than a dozen members.

Analysing these parties is a little like attempting to grasp mercury on a pane of glass. The Eritrean opposition is continually dividing and merging and anything written is often out of date before publication. However, some important themes can be discerned.

Firstly, there is the old division between the ELF and the EPLF (today the PFDJ) that emerged in the 1970s and 80s. Today's parties reflect this political divide.

Secondly, there is a Muslim-Christian fracture. This was always present in the ELF–EPLF divide, but it has been reinforced. Some parties operate from a distinctly Islamist perspective.

Thirdly, there is the ethnic question. Eritrea's nine ethnic groups were not equally represented in the old party hierarchies. The minorities believed themselves to be discriminated against and when the Ethiopia-Eritrea border war was under way (1998–2000) the Ethiopian government assisted in the establishment of ethnically based parties among the Afar and Kunama.

Fourthly, parties have to decide what relationship they will have with Ethiopia. Some embraced the former imperial power while others rejected it. At the same time there is minimal support for the re-incorporation of Eritrea into a greater Ethiopia.

Finally, and perhaps most importantly, there is the relationship between current forms of organisation and the past. The wounds inflicted by the bitter in-fighting amongst Eritrea movements, and the civil war they fought from the 1970s, have been deeply felt and enduring. Eritrea is a small country, with a small population, many of whom knew each other personally. Deaths and torture inflicted on family members have not been forgotten or forgiven, making reconciliation and unity difficult to achieve.

All these issues are well understood by the regime. President Isaias and his colleagues have worked diligently to undermine attempts to resolve differences. Movements have been infiltrated; opposition leaders threatened or bought off. Producing a united opposition has been anything but easy and Eritreans have spent years attempting to do just this. The problem is—at least in part—that many of those who engage in politics abroad bear scars from the past. Old rifts stand in the way of wider unity.

The main movements

Two major movements have emerged, loosely representing the old ELF–EPLF divide. Confusingly, they have similar names.

Sixteen parties founded the Eritrean Democratic Alliance (referred to below as the Alliance) in 2005. (See Appendix 4 for the list of parties that came together in this movement.) Since then other Islamist movements have joined. Most were loosely within the old ELF camp. This in itself caused tensions, with the Alliance dividing into blocs, which had to be reconciled. The Alliance consists of ethnically-based organisations (representing the Kunama and Afar), Islamic-based organisations (like the Eritrean Islamic Reform Movement and the Eritrean Islamic Party for Justice and Development) and the old ELF and its offshoots. The Alliance has held meetings in Sudan and in Ethiopia, where it is now based.

The second movement developed out of a merger between the left wing of the ELF, known as the ELF-Revolutionary Command, and senior party members of the EPLF identified with the G-15 and former journalists and student dissidents who avoided arrest in 2001. The various trends joined to form the Eritrean People's Democratic Party (the Party) in January 2010. Its first chairman was ELF veteran WoldeJesus Ammar. It included within its leadership Mesfin Hagos, a former army commander and a member of the G15 who happened to be outside Eritrea in 2001.

While the Alliance had warm relations with Ethiopia, the Party did not. The Party refused to attend a conference called by the Alliance in Ethiopia in the summer of 2010 at Akaki. The conference was followed by a congress held in the Ethiopian city of Awasa in 2011, which was, in effect, Ethiopia's attempt to launch an Eritrean government in exile. The delegates, who had come from across the world, established yet another movement (the Eritrean National Council for Democratic Change) and elected a legislature of 127 members. But this new body was wracked with differences, which proved insuperable. In December 2015 the Ethiopian government, fed up with the bickering, withdrew funding from the legislature. Ethiopia instead channelled its support through individual parties.

This has not quite killed off the movement. The chairman of the Council, Haj Abdenur, issued a statement in which he announced that a second congress would be held in May 2016. This—he said—would be paid for by Eritreans around the world. But the fracture within the Council is deep: there are fifteen political organisations inside the Council and a further six that are in an opposition camp. Ethiopia has refused to allow the planned congress to take place until their differences can be overcome.

The Alliance and the Party were joined by a third organisation, which was designed to unite previously hostile movements. This was the Forum for National Dialogue, or Medrek. Organized by Andrebrhan Weldegiorgis and other former EPLF leaders, it was said to be a place in which unity could be found in 2013. Speaking at the London launch of the Forum, Dr Assefaw Tekeste, a public health specialist and former head of the EPLF Health Department during the liberation struggle, said their aim was to use their links with people inside the country. 'Our focus is inside Eritrea and we will try to strengthen their hand. We don't want to lead or guide them.' Ambassador Andebrhan told the meeting: 'We are a bridge between the diaspora, who are important, and our colleagues inside Eritrea. But the Forum is led from inside Eritrea.'

Although the Forum has attempted to be an alternative to the other parties or movements, it has fallen foul of many of the same problems. Its leadership is seen as too reminiscent of the old EPLF and some have been accused of being high-handed. A meeting held in Nairobi in 2015 was meant to be a springboard for growth, but like many Eritrean meetings, it ended without achieving its aim.

* * *

The fractious opposition currently poses little threat to the Eritrean government. The divisions within it and their inability to overcome past conflicts and animosities mean they have neither the organisational capacity nor the manpower to challenge President Isaias. At the same time there is no reason why this could not change. There are constant attempts to form new organisations and to bridge previous divides. Eritreans are known for their innovation and tenacity. Why should these skills not be applied to forms of opposition?

One needs to remember that the opposition have an enduring ally in the lowering figure of the president. Isaias Afwerki has never revealed a softer, more accommodating side of his personality. He has been rigidly determined to resist reforms that—in his view—would undermine the security of Eritrea or his grip on power. As long as this stubborn dictator remains in absolute control there will be a stream of fresh recruits for the opposition. Their problem is how to turn them into a real movement to replace the current regime.

11

THE OUTLOOK FOR ERITREA

The political movements can point to only limited achievements. The opposition groups have managed to maintain their presence; they hold regular meetings and continue to challenge the regime via the internet and foreign based radio stations. When the Eritrean authorities attempt to hold public meetings abroad they are now regularly challenged. Demonstrations are held to show that President Isaias no longer retains the affection of large sections of the population. Inside the country only one political party is allowed to operate—the PFDJ, or People's Front for Democracy and Justice. Founded at the third congress of its predecessor (the EPLF) in February 1994, it has never held any form of democratic election. Its 75-strong Central Council and its 19-strong Executive Council are dominated by a single figure: Isaias Afewerki. Like so much of Eritrean life, it is the president who remains the centre of all activity. Much as the opposition would like to challenge his stranglehold on the country, they have so far found no means of doing so.

It was perhaps inevitable that political culture would be weak in a free Eritrea. The brutal history of the movements and the long and bitter struggle for independence militated against the easy development of a vibrant civil society. It required tight, military discipline to sustain the decades of fighting against the Ethiopian government. Orders had to be followed without question—whatever the sacrifice. This culture was reinforced by the Marxism-Leninism of the 1960s and 1970s, which was imbibed by many of the movements, including the EPLF. The party's insistence that Eritrea was a single nation, sometimes denying the ethnic, cultural and religious inclinations of its peoples, strengthened this tendency. Then there were the deep wounds and bitter memories of the civil war between the EPLF and ELF for dominance in the field. Many were killed and internal rifts suppressed. These factors combined to produce a dominant culture that was intolerant of free speech and not conducive to an open, inclusive democracy. The party's formal commitment to these freedoms counted for nothing once independence was achieved.

Having said this, there have always been internal debates, even if they have not been allowed to flourish beyond a narrow circle of the political elite. Once Asmara was liberated in 1991 the tight-lipped secrecy of the war years was gradually eroded, even if the tradition took a while to wear off. By 2000 a lively press had emerged and discussion had began to develop, only to be snuffed out. In exile Eritreans have certainly not been reticent about expressing their views. In person and online there has been a vigorous interchange of ideas, even though these have at times been vituperative and abusive. There is nothing to suggest that a culture of free expression could not thrive inside Eritrea, if it is given the opportunity to do so.

What really stands in the way of the country achieving the democracy it deserves? The obvious answer is President Isaias and his close associates in the military and party. It is they who imprison their opponents, refuse to allow opposition parties to function, implement the Constitution or hold for free and fair elections. Until this obstacle is removed no progress is likely to be made. Yet this is not the whole answer, since it begs further questions.

The president claims that the country is effectively in a state of war with Ethiopia, since Addis Ababa has refused to implement the Boundary Commission's ruling on where the border lies—the issue that sparked off the 1998–2000 conflict. There is some legitimacy in this view. Eritrea is clearly in the right: Ethiopia ought to end its prevarication and implement the Commission's decision as it promised it would. The necessary maps have been supplied to both countries. The ruling has legal force. All that is required is for Ethiopia to recognise its validity.

There have been unconfirmed reports that some members of the international community have been quietly working behind the scenes to try to ensure that this takes place. If it did, tensions between the two neighbours might subside. The Eritrean army could stand down and be reduced to an appropriately small force. The National Service recruits could be demobilised and sent home. Of course this would take time and finance. Releasing tens of thousands of young men and women would leave very substantial numbers unemployed. Eritrea would need help from the international community, which would almost certainly be happy to oblige. They are keen to see stability in the Horn of Africa. For European politicians ending the exodus of Eritreans is a top priority.

The Eritrean government is engaged in a serious attempt to broaden its appeal and to break out of the international isolation in which it finds itself. In this it has allies among the foreign community and the EU states in particular. They are so determined to try to halt the flow of refugees that they are willing to close their eyes to almost any abuses by President Isaias's government. Foreign aid and co-operation are certainly on the table. Despite the repeated failures of previous attempts to 'reset' relations with Asmara, officials in Brussels are determined to continue with these policies. The reports by the UN Human Rights Commission are a setback for these initiatives, especially since the Commission of Inquiry has found evidence of crimes against humanity by the regime. But for the EU they are no more than that: a setback; an obstacle to be overcome.

If sufficient tact, diplomatic leverage and negotiating skill could be deployed to resolve the conflict with Ethiopia then the political climate in the Horn of Africa could be transformed. The ending of the stalemate of 'no war-no peace' would also allow the border to be re-opened. Trade could once more flow between the neighbours, allowing Ethiopia access to Eritrea's ports. Ethiopians would also benefit from this, since Djibouti is struggling to cope with the trade through its port. Eritrea's ports of Assab and Massawa are ideally placed to play this role. They could also play a valuable role in aid operations across the region. In June 2016 the UN's World Food Programme made the first use of Massawa in years when it undertook a trial shipment of 1,100 tonnes of sorghum for South Sudan through the port. For the last decade the WFP came close to ending its relationship with the Eritreans following yet another row with the Isaias government over the distribution of food aid. The ports would need to be rehabilitated and brought back to working order, but this would not be an insuperable obstacle.

Ethiopia has resisted ending the border stalemate since this would require accepting that it has been in the wrong. Instead of showing some flexibility and moving towards reconciliation, the Ethiopian authorities have done exactly the opposite. They have increased tension from time to time by alleging that Eritrea has violated the border in one way or the other. This may, occasionally, have been true, but the tactic is designed to continue the stalemate, which is extremely costly for Eritrea. It is meant to deprive Asmara of the resources it might use to cause trouble for

THE OUTLOOK FOR ERITREA

Addis Ababa. The International Crisis Group believes that there have been at least eight significant flare-ups since 2011, often involving rebel groups sponsored by one or the other of the belligerents. One point is worth underlining: if a full-scale war were to erupt between Ethiopia and Eritrea it is almost certain that the vast majority of the Eritrean diaspora would put their differences with President Isaias aside and rally to the cause. Eritreans of all political persuasions are intensely patriotic. Much the same could be said of Ethiopians, which is why ending this stalemate has proved so intractable.

If a war with Ethiopia can be avoided, but tension on the border continues, then there is little prospect of progress for Eritreans. Politics inside the country is likely to remain frozen. President Isaias and the ruling party would have little reason to allow a cessation of the current repression, since it allows them to remain in place, largely unchallenged. Senior members of the military as well as senior government officials can enjoy the fruits of office with few impediments to their rule.

What might bring this to an end? It would, of course, be possible for the regime to open discussions with the opposition and—gradually—to lift the one-party state, allowing a democratic renewal. Something similar did take place in South Africa, when the apartheid government opened talks with the African National Congress, leading to the release of Nelson Mandela. In the mid-1980s this appeared entirely unlikely, since the country was in flames, yet just five years later the discussions had been held and an agreement had been reached. Nothing can be ruled out, but at the moment there are few signs that Eritrea is about to reach a similar rapprochement. Does Eritrea really have the leaders of the stature of Mandela or de Klerk, who made this transition possible?

As indicated throughout this book, this regime is predicated on Isaias Afewerki. His style of rule is arbitrary, personal and ruthlessly repressive. Former allies and friends have been removed and jailed. Others have been 'frozen' and put out to grass, often at a whim. He has also made large numbers of enemies. The hundreds of thousands who have suffered years of abuse during their National Service or languished in his prisons loathe their leader. There have been at least two attempts to remove him from power by force: once by assassination and once by rebellion. These are incidents that have come to public attention—others may have taken place below the radar. It is certainly possible that despite the care the president exercises over his security that one day this will slip and he will be assassinated. More than twenty African leaders met a similar fate during the previous century.

Predicting such an event is—of course—impossible. Only those intimately involved in any such plot would be in a position to know that it was under way. Even then it could easily fail. What one can legitimately ask is what such a dramatic development might unleash. Many Western nations, as well as powers like China and India, have considerable stakes in the Horn of Africa. All would be concerned that (rather like the Arab Spring) the termination of President Isaias's grip on power might lead to something worse. There have been (and still are) some hardline Islamists among the opposition, but they do not presently represent a major element of the opposition.

The most likely scenario would be that a group within the current hierarchy would take the reins of power—perhaps in a joint administration, involving a leadership council. They would then be in a position to reach out to the opposition movements. An intense dialogue could take place leading to an interim administration and elections. The way would then be open for a legitimate government to be formed, guaranteeing the rights of all citizens.

The nightmare would be at an end. Eritrea could rejoin the international community and take its rightful place among the family of nations. This is an optimistic assessment. One could just as easily paint a much gloomier scenario, involving division, civil strife and years of mayhem. From the current perspective this would appear unlikely. All the opposition can do is maintain their attempts to forge a more effective unity, minimise differences and provide an alternative to the current regime. Together they can keep up the pressure on President Isaias and weaken his attempts to reach out to the rest of the world to reinforce his hold on power. Friends of Eritrea can only wish its people well in this endeavour.

APPENDIX 1

LEADERSHIP OF GOVERNMENT, MILITARY AND PARTY

President Isaias Afewerki
Chairman of the State Council
Chairman of the Transitional National Assembly
C-in-C of the Armed Forces
Chancellor of Institutions of Higher Learning
Chairman of PFDJ
Vice-president vacant since 11/2001

State Council

Ministers

Agriculture	Arefaine Berhe (06/1997–)
Defence	Sebhat Efrem (app. 04/1994)
Education	Semere Russom (04/2007–)
Energy & Mines	Sebhat Efrem (app. 04/2014?)
Finance	Berhane Habtemariam (12/2012)
Fisheries	Tewolde Kelati (01/2010–)
(Marine Resources)	
Foreign Affairs	Usman Saleh (04/2007–)
Health	Amna Nurhusein (03/2009–)
Industry & Trade	Nusredin Ali Bekit (07/2014)
Information	Yemane Gebremeskel (12/2014)

Justice	Fozia Hashim (f) (06/1993–)
Labour and Human Welfare	Kahsai Gebrehiwet (03/2014)
Land, Water and Environment	Tesfai Gebreselasie (03/2009)
Local Government	Weldemikael Abraha (03/2014)
National Development & Economic Co-operation	Dr. Gergish Teklemikael (03/2009–)
Public Works	Abraha Asfaha (1993–)
Tourism	Askalu Menkerios (f) (03/2009–)
Transport & Communication	Tesfaselasie Berhane (03/2014)

Regional Administrators

Anseba	Ali Mahmud (05/2014)
Debub (South)	Efrem Gebrekristos (app. 02/2013)
Debubawi Keyh Bahri (Southern Red Sea)	currently vacant
Gash-Barka	Fisehaye Haile (05/2014)
Ma'ekel (Central)	Major General Romadan Awliya (app. 04/2014)
Semenawi Keyh Bahri (Northern Red Sea)	Tsegereda Weldegergis (f) (11/2008–)

Military Commanders

Navy	MG Mehamed Humed Karikare (1996–)
Air Force	MG Teklay Habteselasie (2002–)
Western Command	BG Tekle Kifle 'Manjus' (04/2014)
Eastern Command	BG Musa Mehamed Rab'a (03/2014)
Southern Command	MG Haile Samuel China (04/2014)

Peoples Front for Democracy and Justice (PFDJ)

Chairman	Isaias Afewerqi (03/1993)
General Secretary	Mehamed Said El Amin (03/1994)

Secretary Political Department	Yemane Gebreab (03/1994)
Secretary Organisational Affairs Department	vacant
Secretary Economic Affairs Department	Hagos Gebrehiwet 'Kisha' (03/1994)
Secretary Research & Documentation Department	Zemehret Yohannes (03/1994)

Transitional National Assembly

Chairman	Isaias Afewerki
Members (06/1997–)	150 (75 PFDJ Central Council. 60 from the 527-member Constituent Assembly 'elected' 1997, 15 representing the diaspora)

High Court

President (Chief Justice)	Mekorios Beraki (08/2001–)

Source: Eritrea Directory, 2016. Kindly provided by a source who wishes to be anonymous. Given the secretive nature of the Eritrean government it is not possible to ensure that this data is entirely accurate or up to date.

APPENDIX 2

US AMBASSADOR RONALD K. MCMULLEN'S
ASSESSMENT OF ISAIAS AFEWERKI, VIA WIKILEAKS

Subject: Bio Notes on Eritrean President Isaias Afwerki

Ref: Asmara 345 'Is Isaias Unhinged?'

By Ambassador Ronald K. McMullen, 5 March 2009

1. (C) Summary: Isaias is an austere and narcissistic dictator whose political ballast derives from Maoist ideology fine-tuned during Eritrea's 30-year war for independence. He is paranoid and believes Ethiopian PM Meles tried to kill him and that the United States will attempt to assassinate him. He is not notably nepotistic and has not favored his ancestral village or immediate family. This message includes some biographic tidbits offered as an addendum to USG bio information on foreign government leaders. End Summary.

2. (C) Aiming for 112: Isaias, 62, told a visiting German parliamentarian in late 2008 that he is healthy and expects to live another 40 or 50 years. He said he hopes to serve his country as long as he is able. In a May 2008 television interview, Isaias said Eritrea might hold elections 'in three or four decades.'

3. (S/NF) An Alleged Ethiopian Assassination Attempt: Isaias and Meles, brothers in arms during the 1980s, are now blood

enemies. Why? In 1996, while returning from a vacation in Kenya, Isaias, his family, and his inner entourage stopped in Addis, where Meles offered to fly them back to Asmara in one of his aircraft. Isaias accepted the offer; en route the aircraft caught fire, but managed to turn back and land safely in Addis. According to someone who was on the aircraft, an infuriated Isaias accuse Meles to his face of trying to kill him and his family. Isaias has not trusted Meles since, according to this source.

4. (S) Fears of an American Assassination Attempt: Isaias thinks the United States will attempt to kill him by missile strike on his residence in the city of Massawa, according to late 2007 information from the Force Commander of UNMEE.

5. (C) Holier Than Thou: Isaias has berated the Chinese ambassador in Asmara for China's embrace of market capitalism. Isaias was sent to China by the Eritrean Liberation Front for political commissar training in the 1960s, where, according to the Chinese ambassador, 'he learned all the wrong things.' Isaias was turned off by the cult of personality surrounding Mao, but apparently internalized Maoist ideology.

6. (C) Fluent in Arabic: Asmara-based Arab ambassadors are impressed by Isaias' fluency in Arabic. There is some debate about where he learned it, but all agree he is a comfortable and capable Arabic speaker.

7. (C) Talented Speechwriter: In mid-2008, after Isaias delivered an impressive address in English to a gathering of ministerial-level representatives on the subject of Darfur, Yemane Ghebremeskel, the director of the office of the president, said Isaias had written the speech himself.

8. (C) Hot Temper: At a January 2008 dinner he hosted for a codel and embassy officials, Isaias became involved in a heated discussion with his Amican legal advisor about some tomato seedlings the legal advisor provided to Isaias' wife. Isaias com-

plained that despite tender care by his wife, the plants produced only tiny tomatoes. When the legal advisor explained that they were cherry tomatoes and were supposed to be small, Isaias lost his temper and stormed out of the venue, much to the surprise of everyone, including his security detail.

9. (C) Holds a Grudge: A senior party official said Isaias and Djibouti President Guelleh had agreed during a 'secure' 2008 telephone conversation to try to resolve at the presidential level issues related to the June border clash. According this senior Eritrean official, Isaias was livid when Guelleh supposedly shortly thereafter lambasted Eritrean aggression in a media interview. Isaias reportedly felt personally betrayed by President Guelleh, and has been obstinate about resolving the Djibouti-Eritrea border dispute ever since.

10. (C) Thin Skinned: Isaias asked to be named the patron of the World Bank-funded Cultural Assets Rehabilitation Project (CARP). When individuals involved with CARP published the book 'Asmara: Africa's Secret Modernist City,' it failed to include a note of thanks to CARP's patron. Isaias was miffed and shut down CARP.

11. (C) Good Op-Sec: Isaias has an aversion to talking on the telephone and frequently sleeps in different locations to foil a coup or assassination attempt. During the winter months he spends most of his time in Massawa rather than in Asmara. When dining in restaurants, Isaias will often switch plates with a subordinate, apparently to avoid being poisoned, according to the Qatari ambassador.

12. (C) The Early Years of Little Beer Pot: Isaias' father, Afwerki, comes from the village of Tselot, which is perched on the lip of a 7,000 escarpment four miles southeast of Asmara. When Isaias was a boy Afwerki reportedly spent much of his time in Tigray, where he owned a coffee farm that was later nationalized by the

Derg. With Afwerki largely absent, Isaias lived with his mother (rumored to have family roots in Tigray) in a working class neighborhood in eastern Asmara near the train depot and the Lutheran church. Isaias' mother made and sold a traditional beer called sewa. By some accounts, Isaias was nicknamed the Tigrinya equivalent of 'Beer Pot,' after the ceramic jug from which sewa is dispensed. Today he is a heavy whisky drinker, but perhaps as a youth his nickname referred as much to his habits as to his mother's business.

13. (C) No Pork for His Ancestral Village: In November 2008 emboffs visited Tselot and saw no indication that the village has received any special favor from Isaias. Like most Eritrean villages, it has electricity but no running water or sewer system. Gaunt cattle and untended donkeys roam the village. Their droppings are quickly gathered and formed into oval patties, which are then stuck on rock walls, dried, and used as fuel for cooking. Afwerki is said to be buried in the village cemetery, but emboffs could not locate his grave. Isaias' immediate family is rarely featured in the state-run media and keeps a low profile. Although his portrait adorns many shops in Asmara, there is no cult of personality in Eritrea. Isaias often appears in the media clad casually in slacks, jacket, open-necked shirt, and sandals or loafers. He rarely travels in a motorcade.

14. (C) Hard-hearted: When a visiting U.S. movie star in early 2008 raised the plight of two Embassy Asmara FSNs who have been imprisoned without charge since 2001, Isaias glared stonily at her and replied, 'Would you like me to hold a trial and then hang them?'

MCMULLEN

APPENDIX 3

ALGIERS AGREEMENT THAT ENDED THE 1998–2000 BORDER WAR BETWEEN ETHIOPIA AND ERITREA

Agreement Between the Government of the Federal Democratic Republic of Ethiopia and the Government of the State of Eritrea

12 December 2000

The Government of the Federal Democratic Republic of Ethiopia and the Government of the State of Eritrea (the 'parties'),

Reaffirming their acceptance of the Organization of African Unity ('OAU') Framework Agreement and the Modalities for its Implementation, which have been endorsed by the 35th ordinary session of the Assembly of Heads of State and Government, held in Algiers, Algeria, from 12 to 14 July 1999,

Recommitting themselves to the Agreement on Cessation of Hostilities, signed in Algiers on 18 June 2000,

Welcoming the commitment of the OAU and United Nations, through their endorsement of the Framework Agreement and Agreement on Cessation of Hostilities, to work closely with the international community to mobilize resources for the resettlement of displaced persons, as well as rehabilitation and peace building in both countries,

Have agreed as follows:

Article 1

1. The parties shall permanently terminate military hostilities between themselves. Each party shall refrain from the threat or use of force against the other.
2. The parties shall respect and fully implement the provisions of the Agreement on Cessation of Hostilities.

Article 2

1. In fulfilling their obligations under international humanitarian law, including the 1949 Geneva Conventions relative to the protection of victims of armed conflict ('1949 Geneva Conventions'), and in cooperation with the International Committee of the Red Cross, the parties shall without delay release and repatriate all prisoners of war.
2. In fulfilling their obligations under international humanitarian law, including the 1949 Geneva Conventions, and in cooperation with the International Committee of the Red Cross, the parties shall without delay, release and repatriate or return to their last place of residence all other persons detained as a result of the armed conflict.
3. The parties shall afford humane treatment to each other's nationals and persons of each other's national origin within their respective territories.

Article 3

1. In order to determine the origins of the conflict, an investigation will be carried out on the incidents of 6 May 1998 and on any other incident prior to that date which could have contributed to a misunderstanding between the parties regarding their common border, including the incidents of July and August 1997.

2. The investigation will be carried out by an independent, impartial body appointed by the Secretary General of the OAU, in consultation with the Secretary General of the United Nations and the two parties.
3. The independent body will endeavor to submit its report to the Secretary General of the OAU in a timely fashion.
4. The parties shall cooperate fully with the independent body.
5. The Secretary General of the OAU will communicate a copy of the report to each of the two parties, which shall consider it in accordance with the letter and spirit of the Framework Agreement and the Modalities.

Article 4

1. Consistent with the provisions of the Framework Agreement and the Agreement on Cessation of Hostilities, the parties reaffirm the principle of respect for the borders existing at independence as stated in resolution AHG/Res. 16(1) adopted by the OAU Summit in Cairo in 1964, and, in this regard, that they shall be determined on the basis of pertinent colonial treaties and applicable international law.
2. The parties agree that a neutral Boundary Commission composed of five members shall be established with a mandate to delimit and demarcate the colonial treaty border based on pertinent colonial treaties (1900, 1902 and 1908) and applicable international law. The Commission shall not have the power to make decisions *ex aequo et bono*.
3. The Commission shall be located in the Hague.
4. Each party shall, by written notice to the United Nations Secretary General, appoint two commissioners within 45 days from the effective date of this Agreement, neither of whom shall be nationals or permanent residents of the party making the appointment. In the event that a party fails to name one or both of its party-appointed commissioners within the

specified time, the Secretary-General of the United Nations shall make the appointment.

5. The president of the Commission shall be selected by the party-appointed commissioners or, failing their agreement within 30 days of the date of appointment of the latest party-appointed commissioner, by the Secretary-General of the United Nations after consultation with the parties. The president shall be neither a national nor permanent resiedent of either party.

6. In the event of the death or resignation of a commissioner in the course of the proceedings, a substitute commissioner shall be appointed or chosen pursuant to the procedure set forth in this paragraph that was applicable to the appointment or choice of the commissioner being replaced.

7. The UN Cartographer shall serve as Secretary to the Commission and undertake such tasks as assigned to him by the Commission, making use of the technical expertise of the UN Cartographic Unit. The Commission may also engage the services of additional experts as it deems necessary.

8. Within 45 days after the effective date of this Agreement, each party shall provide to the Secretary its claims and evidence relevant to the mandate of the Commission. These shall be provided to the other party by the Secretary.

9. After reviewing such evidence and within 45 days of its receipt, but not earlier than 15 days after the Commission is constituted, the Secretary shall transmit to the Commission and the parties any materials relevant to the mandate of the Commission as well as his findings identifying those portions of the border as to which there appears to be no dispute between the parties. The Secretary shall also transmit to the Commission all the claims and evidence presented by the parties.

10. With regard to those portions of the border about which there appears to be controversy, as well as any portions of

the border identified pursuant to paragraph 9 with respect to which either party believes there to be controversy, the parties shall present their written and oral submissions and any additional evidence directly to the Commission, in accordance with its procedures.

11. The Commission shall adopt its own rules of procedure based upon the 1992 Permanent Court of Arbitration Optional Rules for Arbitrating Disputes Between Two States. Filing deadlines for the parties' written submissions shall be simultaneous rather than consecutive. All decisions of the Commission shall be made by a majority of the commissioners.

12. The Commission shall commence its work not more than 15 days after it is constituted and shall endeavor to make its decision concerning delimitation of the border within six months of its first meeting. The Commission shall take this objective into consideration when establishing its schedule. At its discretion, the Commission may extend this deadline.

13. Upon reaching a final decision regarding delimitation of the borders, the Commission shall transmit its decision to the parties and Secretaries General of the OAU and the United Nations for publication, and the Commission shall arrange for expeditious demarcation.

14. The parties agree to cooperate with the Commission, its experts and other staff in all respects during the process of delimitation and demarcation, including the facilitation of access to territory they control. Each party shall accord to the Commission and its employees the same privileges and immunities as are accorded to diplomatic agents under the Vienna Convention on Diplomatic Relations.

15. The parties agree that the delimitation and demarcation determinations of the Commission shall be final and binding. Each party shall respect the border so determined, as well as territorial integrity and sovereignty of the other party.

16. Recognizing that the results of the delimitation and demarcation process are not yet known, the parties request the United Nations to facilitate resolution of problems which may arise due to the transfer of territorial control, including the consequences for individuals residing in previously disputed territory.

17. The expenses of the Commission shall be done equally by the two parties. To defray its expenses, the Commission may accept donations from the United Nations Trust Fund established under paragraph 8 of Security Council Resolution 1177 of 26 June 1998.

Article 5

1. Consistent with the Framework Agreement, in which the parties commit themselves to addressing the negative socio-economic impact of the crisis on the civilian population, including the impact on those persons who have been deported, a neutral Claims Commission shall be established. The mandate of the Commission is to decide through binding arbitration all claims for loss, damage or injury by one Government against the other, and by nationals (including both natural and juridical persons) of one party against the Government of the other party or entities owned or controlled by the other party that are (a) related to the conflict that was the subject of the Framework Agreement, the Modalities for its Implementation and the Cessation of Hostilities Agreement, and (b) result from violations of international humanitarian law, including the 1949 Geneva Conventions, or other violations of international law. The Commission shall not hear claims arising from the cost of military operations, preparing for military operations, or the use of force, except to the extent that such claims involve violations of international humanitarian law.

2. The Commission shall consist of five arbitrators. Each party shall, by written notice to the United Nations Secretary General, appoint two members within 45 days from the effective date of this agreement, neither of whom shall be nationals or permanent residents of the party making the appointment. In the event that a party fails to name one or both of its party-appointed arbitrators within the specified time, the Secretary-General of the United Nations shall make the appointment.

3. The president of the Commission shall be selected by the party-appointed arbitrators or failing their agreement within 30 days of the date of appointment of the latest party-appointed arbitrator, by the Secretary-General of the United Nations after consultation with the parties. The president shall be neither a national not permanent resident of either party.

4. In the event of the death or resignation of a member of the Commission in the course of the proceedings, a substitute member shall be appointed or chosen pursuant to the procedure set forth in this paragraph that was applicable to the appointment or choice of the arbitrator being replaced.

5. The Commission shall be located in The Hague. At its discretion it may hold hearings and conduct investigations in the territory of either party, or at such other location as it deems expedient.

6. The Commission shall be empowered to employ such professional, administrative and clerical staff as it deems necessary to accomplish its work, including establishment of a Registry. The Commission may also retain consultants and experts to facilitate the expeditious completion of its work.

7. The Commission shall adopt its own rules of procedure based upon the 1992 Permanent Court of Arbitration Optional Rules for Arbitrating Disputes Between Two States. All decisions of the Commission shall be made by a majority of the commissioners.

8. Claims shall be submitted to the Commission by each of the parties on its own behalf and on behalf of its nationals, including both natural and juridical persons. All claims submitted to the Commission shall be filed no later than one year from the effective date of this agreement. Except for claims submitted to another mutually agreed settlement mechanism in accordance with paragraph 16 or filed in another forum prior to the effective date of this agreement, the Commission shall be the sole forum for adjudicating claims described in paragraph 1 or filed under paragraph 9 of this Article, and any such claims which could have been and were not submitted by that deadline shall be extinguished, in accordance with international law.

9. In appropriate cases, each party may file claims on behalf of persons of Ethiopian or Eritrean origin who may not be its nationals. Such claims shall be considered by the Commission on the same basis as claims submitted on behalf of that party's nationals.

10. In order to facilitate the expeditious resolution of these disputes, the Commission shall be authorized to adopt such methods of efficient case management and mass claims processing as it deems appropriate, such as expedited procedures for processing claims and checking claims on a sample basis for further verification only if circumstances warrant.

11. Upon application of either of the parties, the Commission may decide to consider specific claims, or categories of claims, on a priority basis.

12. The Commission shall commence its work not more than 15 days after it is constituted and shall endeavor to complete its work within three years of the date when the period for filing claims closes pursuant to paragraph 8.

13. In considering claims, the Commission shall apply relevant rules of international law. The Commission shall not have the power to make decisions *ex aequo et bono*.

14. Interest, costs and fees may be awarded.
15. The expenses of the Commission shall be borne equally by the parties. Each party shall pay any invoice form the Commission within 30 days of its receipt.
16. The parties may agree at any time to settle outstanding claims, individually or by categories, through direct negotiation or by reference to another mutually agreed settlement mechanism.
17. Decisions and awards of the commission shall be final and binding. The parties agree to honor all decisions and to pay any monetary awards rendered against them promptly.
18. Each party shall accord to members of the Commission and its employees the privileges and immunities that are accorded to diplomatic agents under the Vienna Convention on Diplomatic Relations.

Article 6

1. This agreement shall enter into force on the date of signature.
2. The parties authorize the Secretary General of the OAU to register this agreement with the Secretariat of the United Nations in accordance with article 102(1) of the Charter of the United Nations.

DONE at [Algiers, Algeria] on the [12th] day of December, 2000, in duplicate, in the English language.

For the Government of the Federal Democratic Republic of Ethiopia:

[Prime Minister Meles Zenawi]

For the Government of the State of Eritrea:

[President Issaias Afewerki]

APPENDIX 4

ERITREAN DEMOCRATIC ALLIANCE (EDA) (2005)

Founding members EDA

1. Democratic Movement for the Liberation of Eritrean Kunama
2. Eritrean Cooperative Party
3. Eritrean Democratic Opposition Movement (Gash Setit)
4. Eritrean Democratic Party
5. Eritrean Federal Democratic Movement
6. Eritrean Islamic Party for Justice and Development
7. Eritrean Liberation Front (Central Council)
8. Eritrean Liberation Front-National Unity Organisation
9. Eritrean Liberation Front-National Congress
10. Eritrean Liberation Front-Revolutionary Council
11. Eritrean National Democratic Front
12. Eritrean People's Congress
13. Eritrean People's Democratic Front
14. Eritrean People's Movement
15. Eritrean Revolutionary Democratic Front
16. Red Sea Afar Democratic Organisation

BIBLIOGRAPHY

Aid Organization for Refugees and Asylum Seekers in Israel, *Where there is No Free Will—Israel's 'Voluntary Return' procedure for asylum-seekers*, Tel Aviv, April 2015.

Redie Bereketeab, *Eritrea: The Making of a Nation, 1890–1991*, Uppsala: Uppsala University Press, 2000.

Aregawi Berhe, *A Political History of the Tigray People's Liberation Front (1975–1991): Revolt, Ideology, and Mobilisation in Ethiopia*, Los Angeles: African Academic Press, 2009.

Victoria Bernal, 'Equality to Die For?: Women Guerilla Fighters and Eritrea's Cultural Revolution,' *Political and Legal Anthropology Review*, Vol. 23, No. 2: 61–76, November 2000.

Victoria Bernal, 'From Warriors to Wives: Contradictions of Liberation and Development in Eritrea', *Northeast African Studies*, Vol. 8, No. 3: 129–54,. February 2001.

Christopher Clapham (ed.) *African Guerillas*, Oxford: James Currey, 1998.

Dan Connell, *Against All Odds: A Chronicle of the Eritrean Revolution*, Trenton, NJ: Red Sea Press, 1993.

Dan Connell, *Conversations with Eritrean Political Prisoners*, Trenton, NJ: Red Sea Press, 2005.

Dan Connell and Tom Killion, *Historical Dictionary of Eritrea (2nd edn)*, Lanham, MD: Scarecrow Press, 2011.

Martin Doornbos and Alemseged Tesfai (eds), *Post-conflict Eritrea: Prospects for Reconstruction and Development*, Trenton, NJ: Red Sea Press, 1999.

BIBLIOGRAPHY

Mark Duffield and John Prendergast, *Without Troops and Tanks: Humanitarian Intervention in Ethiopia and Eritrea*, Trenton, NJ: Red Sea Press, 1994.

Tekie Fessehatzion, *Shattered Illusion, Broken Promise: Essays on the Eritrea-Ethiopia Conflict (1998–2000)*, Trenton, NJ: Red Sea Press, 2002.

Patrick Gilkes and Martin Plaut, *War in the Horn: The Conflict Between Eritrea and Ethiopia*, London: Chatham House, 1999.

Dawit Wolde Giorgis, *Red Tears: War, Famine and Revolution in Ethiopia*, Trenton, NJ: Red Sea Press, 1994.

Fred Halliday and Maxine Molyneux, *The Ethiopian Revolution*, London: Verso, 1981.

Bereket Habte Selassie, *The Making of the Eritrean Constitution: The Dialectic of Process and Substance*, Trenton, NJ: Red Sea Press, 2003.

Tricia Redeker Hepner, *Soldiers, Martyrs, Traitors and Exiles: Political Conflict in Eritrea and the Diaspora*, Philadelphia, PA: University of Pennsylvania Press, 2009.

Dominique Jacquin-Berdal and Martin Plaut, *Unfinished Business: Eritrea and Ethiopia at War*, Trenton, NJ: Red Sea Press, 1994.

Gaim Kibreab, *Critical Reflections on the Eritrean War of Independence*, Trenton, NJ: Red Sea Press, 2008.

Gaim Kibreab, *Eritea: A Dream Deferred*, Oxford: James Currey, 2009.

Glenys Kinnock, *Eritrea: Images of War and Peace*, London: Chatto & Windus, 1988.

Tekeste Negash and Kjetil Tronvoll, *Brothers at War: Making Sense of the Eritrea-Ethiopian War*, Oxford: James Currey, 2000.

Tekeste Negash, *Eritrea and Ethiopia: The Federal Experience*, Uppsala: Nordiska Africa institutet, 1997.

Roy Pateman, *Eritrea: Even the Stones Are Burning*, Trenton, NJ: Red Sea Press, 1990.

David Pool, *From Guerrillas to Government: The Eritrean People's Liberation Front*, Oxford: James Currey, 2001.

Gerard Prunier and Eloi Ficquet (eds) *Understanding Contemporary Ethiopia: Monarchy, Revolution and the Legacy of Meles Zenawi*, London, Hurst, 2015.

Richard Reid (ed.), *Eritrea's External Relations: Understanding its Regional Role and Foreign Policy*, London: Chatham House, 2009.

BIBLIOGRAPHY

Ravinder Rena, 'Women in Eritrea: Reflections from Pre and Post Independence Period', *The Indian Journal of Labour Economics*, Vol. 50, No. 2: 357–70, June 2007.

Filip Reyntjens, *The Great African War: Congo and Regional Geopolitics, 1996–2006*, New York, Cambridge University Press, 2009.

Amare Tekle (ed.), *Eritrea and Ethiopia: From Conflict to Cooperation*, Trenton, NJ: Red Sea Press, 1994.

Kjetil Tronvoll, *The Lasting Struggle for Freedom in Eritrea: Human Rights and Political Development, 1991–2009*, Oslo: Oslo Centre for Peace and Human Rights, 2009.

Kjetil Tronvoll, *Mai Weini: A Highland Village in Eritrea*, Trenton, NJ: Red Sea Press, 1998.

United Nations Commission of Inquiry on Human Rights in Eritrea Reports, http://www.ohchr.org/EN/HRBodies/HRC/CoIEritrea/Pages/commissioninquiryonhrinEritrea.aspx, last accessed 23 August 2016.

United Nations Security Council, Somalia and Eritrea Sanctions Committee, Monitoring Group Reports, https://www.un.org/sc/suborg/en/sanctions/751/work-and-mandate/reports, last accessed 23 August 2016.

Andebrhan Welde Giorgis, *Eritrea at a Crossroads: a Narrative of Triumph, Betrayal and Hope*, Houston: Strategic Book Publishing, 2014.

Peter Woodward, *The Horn of Africa: Politics and International Relations*, London: I.B. Tauris, 2003.

Wolde-Yesus Ammar, *Eritrea: Root Causes of War and Refugees*, Baghdad: Sindbad Publishing, 1992.

Michela Wrong, *I Didn't Do It For You: How the World Betrayed a Small African Nation*, London and New York: Fourth Estate, 2005.

John Young, *Armed Groups Along Sudan's Eastern Frontier: An Overview and Analysis*, London: Small Arms Survey, 2007. http://www.small-armssurveysudan.org/fileadmin/docs/working-papers/HSBA-WP-09-Eastern-Frontier.pdf, last accessed 23 August 2016.

John Young, *The Tigray People's Liberation Front, 1975–1991*, Cambridge: Cambridge University Press, 1997.

Bahru Zewde, *The Quest for Socialist Utopia: The Ethiopian Student Movement, c. 1960–1974*, Woodbridge: James Currey, 2014.

INDEX

INDEX

INDEX

INDEX

INDEX

INDEX

INDEX

INDEX

INDEX

INDEX